A Leap of Faith

RESOURCE GUIDE FOR FOSTER CARE AND ADOPTION

JILL NORTON

aBM

A Leap of Faith

Published by:
A Book's Mind
PO Box 272847
Fort Collins, CO 80527
www.abooksmind.com

ISBN 978-1-939828-88-0

Table of Contents

Introduction

"That Our God may count you worthy of His calling, and that by His power He may fulfill every good purpose of yours and every act prompted by your faith. We pray this so that the name of our Lord Jesus may be glorified in you." 2 Thessalonians 1:11-12 [NIV]

The bible says that children are a blessing from the Lord, and blessed is the man whose quiver is full. We are incredibly blessed people! Our quiver is no doubt full. We have had many years with the pitter-patter of little feet. Laughter has filled the walls of our home on many occasions. Bringing the children into our life was a leap of faith that turned into a daily walk of faith. It was sometimes very difficult. But, we have had the privilege of seeing physical, emotional, and spiritual healing take place in them.

We truly are blessed, and thank God that he chose us — two willing, but inadequate people, to care for His children. I was never voted the most gifted person, or the one most likely to succeed. I have learned a secret, it's a place where ordinary people do extraordinary things. I can do all things through Christ who strengthens me. Without Him, none of this would have been possible. He is the one who *replaces the years the locust have eaten*. He is a *Father for the fatherless*. He is *close to the broken hearted and those who are crushed in spirit*. He is the *healer of our souls*. We thank Him for giving us the strength, wisdom, and heart's desire to care for the lesser of these…His children!

In the following pages, I have been very honest concerning the challenges, and blessings of bringing eight foster children—all of different ages and backgrounds—into our heart and home and eventually adopting them. I want this book to be positive and at the same time I want it to be real. That was sometimes difficult for me. As I was writing concerning some situations we have encountered, it didn't seem too positive, but I felt it needed to be talked about, because it is true. I will share what it was like when the kids entered our home, and what issues we have had to deal with, with each individual child. I realize now the issues we have, and continue to deal with, are very common when dealing with foster children. I know we are not alone.

More than just sharing my story with you, I will also address how the system works. How we manage a birth family, and why birth family connections are so important to kids that are in the system. Not monetary, but what has this cost us in our daily lives, as well as how we discipline. And my favorite chapter: *Things you need to know*, which is filled with many tips on how to make your journey through foster care and adoption a more successful one.

My desire is that this book will encourage those who have ever thought about the possibility of foster care and/or adoption, to possibly take that final step and give a child a home they so desperately need. For those of us who have been brave enough to do it, I hope you will also find encouragement and maybe some ideas that will be helpful to you in your journey—as I will share what has and has not worked for our family.

In the book, I have used fictitious names for the kids for their protection and privacy.

I also want to thank William "Bill" Owsley, Dependency Division Chief in the office of the Legal Advocate, for taking time out of his busy schedule to let me rack his brain, and give me the information I needed for the chapter called, *Understanding the System*.

Bill, and his wife Hollie, have been great friends to Tom and me since meeting them 11 years ago when this journey first began. Bill has a heart for kids in the system, and works long and hard to ensure that they are never overlooked. He has been, and continues to be, an inspiration to our family.

I want to dedicate this book to my husband, my best friend, my laughing and crying buddy, my greatest encourager, my better half—the one who knows me and loves me anyway. There is no one else I would have rather walked this journey with than you! It has been fun, it has been hard, and it isn't over yet! Glad we get to finish it together, until death do us part. I love you, Babe!

A note from family and friends

"So brothers and sisters, since God has shown us great mercy, I beg you to offer your lives as a sacrifice to Him. Your offering must be only for God and pleasing to Him, which is the spiritual way for you to worship." Romans 12:1 [NVC]

"We became fast friends with Tom and Jill, after meeting at church in 1991. Both newly married with young children, and like-minded personalities, it was a perfect recipe for a lifelong friendship that would endure the wonderful and difficult stages of life as young adults, married with children. I have always felt a special connection with Jill. She is more like my sister, rather than just my friend. So, when my precious friend called with a prayer request in 2001, I could hear the panic in her voice, and sense the terror in her heart—even though she was attempting, with all her might, to conceal it.

We were about to embark upon a new and exciting *season* of life. Our children were just about ready to leave home for college. We were almost *empty nesters*. That meant travel, date night any day of the week, and walking around the house in just our skin whenever we felt like it—mid-life adult freedom! Jill wasn't panicked because her boys were about to leave home, or over *empty nesters'* excitement. God was calling her and Tom into a ministry of foster–adopt parenting. God was calling, but Jill wasn't sure she wanted to answer. My friend was being called into a life-changing sacrificial ministry, and she needed prayer.

I love Jill, and I felt her panic inside of my own body after we hung up the phone, so I began to pray immediately. God not only answered my prayer—and those of many others—He began to rain down His glory upon the Norton's household, and has continued doing so ever since.

Tom and Jill Norton suit up and show up to God's calling upon their lives every single day, whether they feel like it or not. They have glorified God in the process of becoming parents to eight beautiful adopted children. What an amazing honor and privilege God has so graciously given me, to witness, with my own eyes, what Godly obedience looks like; and what a vast array of heavenly blessings God pours out upon those who surrender their lives completely to Him. There is so much of *God's glow* around them that when someone, like me, brushes up against it, I receive residual blessings in the process. Tom and Jill are living out—Romans 12:1. Watching them in action renews and strengthens my faith in ways I could never have imagined. Their living testimony causes my heart to leap for joy, and to burst into worship and praise for the One who made it all possible.

Sometimes, God bestows enormous wealth upon an individual in the form of friendship. I am such a person. Thank you Tom and Jill for your obedience and sacrifice to our Lord and Savior Jesus Christ. I am truly blessed to call you both my friend."

— Erin Bellah / Friend of the family

Thank you for your call upon the Norton's lives. Thank you for giving them a heart to love children who are unloved, for nurturing children who have been abused, for holding children who have been frightened and neglected, for feeding the unfed, clothing the unclothed, providing medical care for the sick and crying for their souls. They have been faithful in their calling, even when it was difficult. You have given them strength in their weariness, and love to take in just one more child. Help them to remember in the dark what they knew in the light. Thank you for the gift I have in their friendship, and watching their faithfulness. Thank you for this peek into the kingdom and the opportunity to encourage them and the privilege of praying for them.

— Cheri Sanders / Friend and psychologist

"Jill and Tom Norton have been bringing their foster children to me, for pediatric care, for about ten years. They have cared for children from many backgrounds and with a wide variety of unique problems. These have included developmental delay, failure to thrive (inadequate growth), asthma, eating disorders (including food hoarding), and obesity. Under their care, these foster children have flourished, been taught healthy eating habits, and have been in a stable and loving environment. One of their adopted children, who was initially obese, lost one hundred pounds in the first ten months, just by being placed on a sensible eating plan with healthy portion sizes, no seconds, and no soda.

People often talk about *nature versus nurture* in the context of raising children, as if children turn out either *good* or *bad* based solely on one or the other. I know that in the Norton family, each child is affected by his or her unique nature, but is in the most nurturing environment possible.

Raising children, especially foster children, requires patience and a true desire to better the child's life. Tom and Jill have both of these qualities, and years of experience raising foster children. They speak from experience."

— Thomas Brousseau MD

"I first met the Norton family when I had their son Mike in my first grade classroom. Mike was a bit shy, but soon fit right in with all the other first grade boys enjoying chasing, playing anything with a ball, and joining in the first grade activities. He also invited me to a piano recital he was in since his parents had him take lessons. Since Mike, I have also had Cindy, Cathy, Joy, and Mara come through my first grade classroom over the years. With each child, Jill was a very involved mom. She was my room mother each year I had one of the children, and she came in for weekly (and sometimes daily) reports of how each of the children were doing both academically and socially in school. I wish all my student's parents would be so involved. Jill always wanted to know how she could help if any of the children were having a problem with schoolwork.

Having five of the children allowed the Norton's and me ample time to form a friendship, and I have been invited to their home for dinner several times. As I arrived, I always saw both Tom and Jill sitting with each of the children at their huge kitchen table working on homework, explaining and re-teaching things that needed attention, and checking to make sure each of the children not only completed all homework assignments, but understood all the concepts taught that day.

Feeding ten mouths for dinner every day can't be easy, yet Tom and Jill pull it off without a hitch. They have taught each of the children how to pitch in and work together as a family. The children each have their own chores, and take turns doing *dish duty* each evening. This is amazing to watch!

Are there problems? Of course, they all are human. But the lessons of accountability, a good work ethic, and the absence of an entitlement mentality, coupled with a spirit of gratefulness for all their blessings instilled in the children by Tom and Jill have offset many problems.

But what truly binds this family together in love for each other is their close relationship and reliance on the Lord. This family is a model of how knowing Christ instills love for others."

— Jan Musser / Teacher at Grace Lutheran School

"What a ministry God has led Tom and Jill into! I remember the excitement Jill exhibited when she told me they were fostering their first child. God had laid it on their hearts to give a home and their love to one who especially needed it.

Soon it was not one child, but two…and before long, they were asked to give loving homes to others. Three…four…five…six … "NO MORE"…oops. Two more needed a home and Tom and Jill just couldn't say, "No."

Early on, they also determined to give the children some stability and security by officially adopting them, and making them part of their forever family.

With the support of their biological sons Ted and Matt, Jill and Tom have gone through the highs and lows of welcoming into their homes and lives the young ones who had been through so much emotional and sometimes physical trauma. They have shown such strength. So often Jill's conversation began with, "Tom and I have prayed about…" Then she would continue, sometimes with laughter, but often near tears with genuine concern. Only with the definite leading of the Lord and His gifts of wisdom, strength, patience, and love could they have made it through.

Struggles? Definitely! Tears? Yes! Fatigue? Daily! Joys? Many! The young ones have learned that because of their unconditional love, "Mom and Dad Norton" are not going to abandon them for any reason. What a wonderful example of what our Heavenly Father gives to us who have been adopted into his family!"

— Eunice Holbert / Friend of Jill's for 44 years

"We were 14 and 16 years old when our parents brought in the first of many kids. We were not surprised because the decision to bring in foster kids was a family decision. Our parents never brought in kids without discussing it with us first. We had no idea, and neither did they for that matter, how many kids would end up finding a family with us.

When Cindy and Cathy moved in, we were really happy. We liked kissing their baby cheeks, and it was fun watching Cindy become a real child because it was such a miraculous thing. It didn't seem to change the family atmosphere much. I remember Mom and Dad being worried that they weren't spending as much time with us, but we weren't bothered by that. They would take us out on dates, and leave the girls at home. We would be mad that they didn't include the girls in the date.

It really has been a team effort. Both of us have had to bring different things to the table to also make this work smoothly. We have babysat for Mom and Dad on numerous occasions. In all seriousness, we care for these kids as if they were our very own siblings. We would do anything for them.

We have heard different people say to Mom and Dad that it really hasn't been fair to us. We had to sacrifice time with our parents, room, and privacy, and really give up the only family we had ever known. We say that it has helped us realize that life is not about us and that there is joy in giving. We watch so many people of faith do nothing with their faith. We have watched Mom and Dad put their faith into action, and it has helped us to see who Jesus really is. Our parents have been the tools that God has used to help these kids get better.

It has only been hard when we have seen our parents struggle. We have watched them go through some difficult times with the kids, as well as take insults from some people on the outside looking in. We have hated that part of it. Everyone has an opinion, but most have no idea what goes on.

It was kind of hard, and a rude awakening, when Paul and Sarah both moved in because they both have disabilities that are hard to live with. You want to help them, and help your parents help them, but you don't have any idea what to do.

Ted and I have always been really close, but Mom and Dad had to pour so much of their lives into these kids it made the two of us even closer. (Matt says) There have been transitional moments in my life where I felt there was a cost at bringing them in. At the same time, having eight kids grieve for me when I was going through tremendous pain made the cost go away. I realized it was all worth it, and we were a true family. We laugh together, cry together, and really truly care about each other.

We feel like nothing really changed as each new child was brought in, it was just another face with each additional child. Matt moved out at 18, so he wasn't living here when Sarah, Paul, or David moved in.

We have been living with these kids so long that looking back, the kids have always been here. We like having the big family, except when it's family picture time. That is the most miserable time of the year.

In conclusion, we both think our family *ROCKS*!

Mom and Dad, we think you are awesome!"

— Matthew and Theodore (Teddy) Norton

"Writing this from the perspective of being Tom and Jill's pastor and friend, the truest and best thing that my wife and I could share would be that Tom and Jill are not perfect. Well, that is not a very kind thing to write, you may be saying. We write it only with the knowledge that they would say the very same thing. But, here is the key, they know, intimately, the One who is perfect, and depend wholly upon Him while caring for the children he has given to them.

We have had the privilege to have a very small part of that experience. We were there for the adoption of the very first two girls, the heart-wrenching dedication of the child they were unsure they would be allowed to care for, and loved so deeply, to the continued acceptance of the other children the Lord offered them—and, of course, the precious rejoicing as each child chose to enter into a relationship with Jesus and, subsequently be baptized in the family pool announcing to the world their choice to follow Jesus. Because of this, we can honestly say that Tom and Jill's primary focus has been on raising His children in the nurture and admonition of the Lord.

As we alluded to earlier, they began this process with each child dedicating them to the Lord. They gave back to Him what he had given so sweetly to them. They did this as a wonderful family-and-friend celebration that we were privileged to take part in, and I to officiate. Each child knew that the primary blessing these people could give to them as their new parents, was revealing Jesus and His amazing grace to them. They knew that they were indeed special, not because they had a nice new house, a cute bedroom, toys, or cute outfits to wear. No, they were special because they belonged to the Lord, and that was worth celebrating.

Not only were we allowed to participate in the celebrations, but also in their struggles. Tom and Jill were real and willing to share with us the difficult situations life brought with each child. In that realness was a vulnerability to seek counsel and ask for prayer. Yes, they became more aware of their own frailties and insecurities that revealed themselves as different child-related/family-related struggles arose. We would talk and pray through these situations. But at this point, we must all be asked the question, "How would we, or any of these children, ever know of the **grace of God** if sin, trials, temptation never entered the world?"

Even though we dedicate our lives to the Lord, it does not immune us from struggles. What we choose to do, whom we choose to turn to during those struggles, makes all the difference in the world. His word promises us that if we ask for wisdom, He will give in abundance. We have seen the Lord walk with them, and see them through each difficulty, giving them the wisdom that they need. That wisdom may have been direction for discipline, an opportunity for teaching, to seek forgiveness, or simply showing grace. We have witnessed

God's blessing in their celebrations and their struggles and each time, whether good times or hard times, God was magnified and glorified in this family.

So we again state, Tom and Jill are not perfect, their children are not perfect. But this we know, life is not about perfection; it is about living a life laid down to the will of the Father, growing in the grace and knowledge of His son, Jesus Christ, and exalting His almighty name. Tom, Jill, and their amazing family do this very well. To God be the glory!"

— Pastor Mike Benjamin of Calvary Community Church, Phoenix, and his precious wife, Tammy

"I remember when Jill came to us and told us they were thinking about fostering a couple of little girls.

Our first thought was fear. We knew that it would change a lot of things for them. We knew that they were getting older, and we wondered how they would retire with kids still in the house. Being older, we knew that there comes a time when you don't want to do some of things you did when you were younger. Our concern was them getting burned out. Jill's boys were also getting older and I was looking forward to spending more time alone with Jill. I didn't know how bringing in little ones would affect our time together as mother and daughter.

When they got the first two little girls, of course we thought they were precious and we became Grandma and Grandpa very quickly.

With each additional child, it became easier. We knew Tom and Jill had a heart for children, but we reminded them that they couldn't save the world.

When you first bring children into your home that are not your biological children, you don't really realize how each child comes with their own baggage. We have tried to be supportive and helpful to Tom and Jill as the struggles with the kids have come to light.

It also has to be hard for the children coming into a new environment where there is now structure and discipline. We have also tried to be there for the kids. They are always welcome at Grandma and Grandpa's house, and we really love them like they were our own grandchildren. They have also accepted us as their grandparents and are very loving towards us. It is a lot of fun getting us all together for dinner or holidays.

We feel these children are very blessed to be taught all the life skills that will be so important in their lives later on. We think Tom and Jill have done a great job with each of them."

— Grandma and Grandpa Haupt

"We have known the Norton family since the mid 90's. Our children attended the same grade school together. Tom was just getting a retirement business started, Jill was babysitting, and Mary and I were teaching and coaching.

Jill is very outgoing, and somewhere along the way, we were invited to spend time with them on date nights, and on family outings. We have become very close over the years, sharing crazy fun times and some tears too..

Together, we continued to watch our kids grow, cheer for them in sporting events, sing songs around campfires, and take some beatings on a tube pulled behind the Norton's boat. Great times!

In the meantime, Tom's business flourishes and we all see the Lord showering them with blessings. Having been convicted in their hearts, they knew they were going to share their blessings with others. One date night they ran an adoption scenario by us. My wife and I look at each other and asked them if they had prayed about it, which they had, and we said the idea was a great one, a challenging one, but a great one.

Of course, they sought the advice of family members and church members and friends, all whom encouraged them to pray about it and to think beyond the *here and now* and to consider the long-term ramifications. All of these people continue to this day to support Tom and Jill emotionally and spiritually.

As I mentioned before, Jill is very outgoing and Tom, he is an adventurous risk taker. Now, with this combination of personality traits we have the perfect marriage for successful foster care and adoption. It's definitely a risky venture. You can almost hear the theme music from *Jaws* playing in your head as you wait to see how things unfold. Who would show up in their home? How many would show up? How would they respond to their new home? What role would or could we play?

So it was that Cindy and Cathy came to be with the Norton's. Two little baby girl sisters in need of stability. Whew, that wasn't so tough. Camping trips (one that Matt, Ted, and Jesse will never forget) and date nights continued. Of course, the system checks in on the welfare of the girls, and sees that they are thriving, so they ask the family to take on another child, a little boy, Mike. Their hearts are wide open, and Mike is welcomed in. Mike has an infant baby sister who needs a home. Well, we thought she was an infant because she looked like she was six weeks old, but she was almost seven months old. Hearts broke for Joy and she became family. Tom and Jill are a couple with more compassion and grace than anyone either myself or my wife has ever met. We are actually in awe of lives being touched and events unfolding.

We're only half way there, now comes Mara, Paul and Sarah, and then David. Are our friends crazy? No, quite the opposite, it is their faith-based trust in the Lord that has brought them together with these children. We are blessed to be a part of it all. We even get *adopted* along the way as Uncle Paul and Aunt Mary. What a privilege.

As uncle and aunt, we have been able to create opportunities to spend time with the kids. We share what we love with them. I'm an avid reader, and from the time Mara was a baby big enough to sit up, she would let me read to her. I'm a lifetime wrestler, and have shared that with Mike, Paul, and David. Mary also enjoys planning activities for all the kids. A field trip to the Rosen House with Cindy, Cathy, and Sarah, a trip to the movies to see *Iron Man* with the boys, at home movie and puzzle fun with Joy and Mara. A great way to enjoy a summer day would be at Camp Whitson with pool relay games, and diving for coins. Most recently, a Christmas scavenger hunt that included shaving cream, Santa beards, and reading the Christmas story from the book of Luke to a stranger, made some special memories.

But, our most coveted time is the time at the cabin with no time restraints or schedule. We play softball, badminton, volleyball, and best of all, Frisbee golf. Mary and the kids bake goodies, try new soup recipes, make jewelry, put together puzzles, and play card games. Board games like *Malarkey* reveal which kids have the ability to fashion a believable *untruth* with a straight face.

You find out who the most competitive ones are, and who is just there for the fun and laughter. Some just like their books to read, but even a reader can have fun with the card game *Spot It*. It's quick, it's loud, and there is a lot of laughter! There is nothing like the laughter of the Norton kids!

We are grateful to be a part of the adventures of the Norton family. We hope the kids know they are loved by their aunt and uncle, and that the time spent with them is important to us."

— Uncle Paul and Aunt Mary Whitson / Tom and Jill's best friends

Where it all began

My husband Tom and I met in 1981 while we were both working at a fast food restaurant, Jack in the Box. I was a senior in high school, and he was attending a university nearby. The moment we met, we connected. Tom asked me to go play racquetball one night with him. I accepted his invitation. After that date, I went home and told my mom I had met the man I was going to marry. She thought I was cute, didn't think much about it, until five months later when I came home with a ring on my finger.

We spent the next year planning a small, but beautiful, church wedding. We got married on a lovely October evening in front of all our family and friends. We didn't have much money, and neither of us had any time off work, so we spent our honeymoon in Tucson, Arizona walking around Old Tucson. My dad worked for a hotel chain, and as a wedding gift, he got us the honeymoon suite at one of his hotels in Tucson. It was more than we would have been able to afford.

Our first apartment was a duplex about half a mile from where I grew up. I can remember purchasing our first couch at a Goodwill store for eighty dollars. It about broke us. We had one car that I used to get to work, while my husband took the bus downtown to his job at a bank.

I had a lot to learn about being a wife, and taking care of a husband. I was barely nineteen years old. I remember when I was a young lady, my mom telling me I needed to stay home and help her with preparing meals for the family because one day I would be married and would need to know how to cook. She probably was right, but I had no interest in cooking. I just wanted to run down the street and hangout with my best friend. I was hoping my husband would be able to cook some, or we would both either live off Top Ramon noodles—or love. Besides, I figured I wouldn't be married for years.

I did get married sooner than later, and couldn't even cook an egg—let alone a chicken dinner. But we had fun figuring it out together.

We spent the first two years of marriage planning for the future. We wanted to buy a house, and start a family, so we decided to save all of my paychecks for two years, and then we went house hunting.

We eventually found a house we could afford. It was a three bedroom, one bath, house a few miles away, and we decided to buy it. We were so excited! We added on a fireplace, a laundry room, and a back porch. We remodeled the living room and bedroom. We painted the outside of the house, and tore down dead trees. We loved our little house. It only had swamp cooling, so for a month or two in the summer when there was a lot of humidity we would melt, but we made it through. The house also had a lot of roaches and some mice. We set traps, and killed bugs, but we were happy. It was our home.

Two years after moving into our love-nest, we got pregnant with our first son. He was born the end of July, 1986. I don't like needles, and so I wouldn't let my husband take me to the hospital until a few hours before he was born. I had him naturally, and everything went smoothly. There is such a miracle in giving birth to another life. I will never forget when we first laid eyes on our precious little boy. He had strawberry-blonde hair just like his daddy. He arrived in this world with his eyes wide open, and not a sound coming out of his mouth. We were immediately in love. We named him Matthew.

We took him home, and adjusted to a new life with the three of us. I continued working until he was a year old, and then I decided to stay home with him and provide daycare to other working parents so I could still help my husband with the expenses.

Matthew was a good baby. He was Daddy's little boy. He was very smart, and compliant, an easy child. He spoke early, and very clearly. He was walking by nine months, and He could ride a two-wheel bike by age three. He was a typical first-born child.

A little over a year later, we decided to have another child. I was hoping for a girl. My husband's twin brother had two girls, and so I figured we would have the two boys, but I was still hoping for a girl. It didn't take long to conceive, and before long, our second son, Teddy was born.

The doctor said, "You have a son."

I replied, "Oh Shoot."

Believe me, I have lived with that for years. My husband likes to tease me about it, and to this day the whole family knows that Mama's first words when her second son was born was not, "Oh how precious," it was instead, "Oh Shoot."

Teddy was born in October of 1988. One hour and 47 minutes away from our sixth wedding anniversary. Unlike his brother, he came into the world screaming, and he didn't stop. He was a hard child. He cried a lot as an infant, and when he was able to get around on his own, he had a mind of his own. He was more defiant than his big brother, and more of a risk taker.

The boys were total opposite, but the best of buds. Teddy had no fear, and Matt was very fearful, so Ted got Matt to come out of his shell some. I had to look at Matt cross, and he would stop any negative behavior, but Ted didn't care how I looked at him. If he wanted to do something, he was going to do it, and worry about the consequences later.

When Ted was two, we moved into our second house. It was a four-bedroom house with air conditioning. We were thrilled. It didn't have any roaches or mice. We were moving up.

The boys continued to grow, and they stayed very close. Even when we informed them that they could have their own rooms, they opted to room together. They did everything together. They started mowing neighbors' lawns together, and got their first job at the same pizza place when they each turned sixteen years old. They went to the prom together with their girlfriends. They were inseparable, and still are to this day.

They both attended a small Lutheran school a few miles away. Tom and I began volunteering our time at their school. We loved it. We knew all their friends, and their friends' parents. The boys played all the school sports: softball, soccer, cross country, basketball, and track.

We spent a lot of time at the lake. We bought a ski boat, and took friends out to ski and inner tube all summer. We also loved to go camping, hiking, and vacationing as a family. We were really active. We enjoyed being parents, but the two of them made it easy on us.

We got through their high school years smoothly. They both were good students. They were also in a band with some friends from church, and so that kept them busy. They were respectful, and obedient—typical teenagers though. A night of fun to them was filling a cooler full of water balloons, and driving around throwing them at unsuspecting victims. I guess harmless stuff (we found out about that years later).

I continued to provide daycare so that I was always home for the boys. In 1999, my husband decided to start his own business. He had been working for a bank in town for years. He wanted to step out and see how he did on his own. It would eventually be one of the greatest blessings to our family, and it also enabled us to be involved with taking in foster children.

Throughout the years of our marriage, we were also very involved in our church. We led children's worship for a while, and then moved on to teach Sunday school for years. Tom and I were both raised in Christian homes, and our faith was very important to us, and it was the foundation of our lives together as a family.

As our boys got a little older, we realized how quickly time goes by. Tom and I didn't want to get to the end of our lives and wish we had done more to make a difference in the lives of others. Up until then, we had volunteered in school, and taught Sunday school, but that wasn't much. We believed that faith meant action, and that God had a plan and a purpose for our lives. We began to pray that God would lay on our hearts a specific ministry, and that whatever he called us to do, we would do.

After praying for a couple of years, Tom and I realized that God was calling us to bring into our home children that had been abused and neglected. God had given us a heart's desire to be a voice for the weak, and an instrument or tool in the hand of God that would be used in the lives of children.

There were many things to consider. We needed to talk this over with our boys, and some of our extended family. I know that God didn't only call Tom and me, he also called our boys to this ministry, as well as some of our extended family.

Some of the questions we had to consider: 1) Would our extended family support this decision? 2) What if we brought into our home a child of a different race? We sat down and talked to the boys about it first. They were very positive, and they supported—and were genuinely excited about the possibility of bringing some children into our home.

Our parents were a little more apprehensive. My parents didn't want us giving up our later years by having to raise kids. They shared with us that you age differently between 40 to 50 years old then you do between 30 and 40 years old. They didn't think we would be interested with kids as we got older. They thought we should spend those years traveling, eating out, watching the boob tube, and visiting with other "old" people. I was still in my 30's at the time, and Tom was in his early 40's. We didn't feel that old.

Tom's parents didn't say anything. They just stared at us. We didn't know how to take that reaction, so we didn't do or say anything else. It was quite unusual, but understandable. It is a scary decision for some, and they don't know what to say.

We spent a lot of time talking and sharing with them our heart's desire. We also explained what we were learning about kids in the system, and how desperately they needed homes. We wanted them to understand why we were making the decision to bring these precious lives into our home. It didn't take long before they were also excited, and looking forward to being a part of whatever the future had in store for us all.

We contacted an agency in the Phoenix area, and we began what was a very long process. We had to provide personal references, pass criminal background checks, get a physician's statement verifying our emotional and physical health, we had to prove we had adequate income to support our own family's needs as well as have adequate space for a foster child. There were many home visits, tons of paperwork, fingerprints, CPR classes, along with 30 hours of intense training to *prepare us* for what lay ahead. After our paperwork was turned into the state, we waited a few months before being notified that they had lost our file. It was frustrating, but we had already been praying for a couple of years, and so we continued to pray that God would bring to us the children that he had picked for our family.

During the process of receiving a license for foster care, we began fixing up a room for two more children. At the time, we were not looking for a new home. The home we had, had already passed the state's inspection for foster children. One Sunday while I was at church, I met another woman who was also working in Children's ministry. We began to talk, and we became fast friends. Their family invited our family over for a Fourth of July get together.

While we were at their house, we noticed that the house next door to them was for sale. For some reason, my husband wanted to inquire about it. I wasn't sure why since we were both perfectly content with the house we lived in. He did inquire, and we ended up making them an offer that they accepted.

The house we were in had four small bedrooms, and two bathrooms. The new house had five large bedrooms, three bathrooms, and huge living spaces. So, it was considerably larger than the home we had. What we didn't realize at the time was that God's plan for us was much bigger than two more children. He brought us to this new home, in His timing, for His purpose. Had we been able to see into the future, we probably would have gotten a little frightened at what was about to unfold.

Once our paperwork was passed through, and our new house inspected, we were finally *accepted* by the state. We received our license to do foster care for children in the state of Arizona. The process took us ten months to complete. The next step was to have a meeting with our new licensing worker.

Our licensing worker came over on October 1. She asked us what ages of children we were willing to take. Because it was our first placement, and we had heard several *horror stories* about how these kids are messed up, we decided to only take children newborn through age three. We wanted girls because we had two boys, and my husband grew up with six brothers, no sisters, and so he wanted to know what it was like to have girls in the house. She informed us that it would take some time, maybe even six months. We were all right with that. She left, and we went back to our daily chores.

An hour later, I was playing the piano when our phone rang. It was our licensing worker. She informed us that after she left our house she went directly back to her office. She had just received paperwork that showed all children available for placement that week. On the list, she noticed a little girl, age 13 months, and her older sister, who was almost three. She said they were just put into the system, and that we should call their worker at Child Protective Services to see if they would place the children with us. This is where it all began....

Cindy and Cathy

We moved into our new home in the heat of the summer. On August 15, 2002, we were blessed with the keys so we could begin the horrible task of packing everything up and moving.

We had received the phone call from our licensing worker about the girls on October 1. We immediately called the CPS (Child Protective Service) case-worker to find out more information regarding the girls. She told us that they were both in *emergency receiving placements*. The youngest child, Cathy, would be available to be placed in a week. Her older sister, Cindy, would be available in two weeks. Cindy had multiple doctor appointments, and so they wanted to leave her in her original placement until those appointments had been completed.

The worker then gave us some background information on the girls. She told us that their birth mother had left the two girls in the care of her family, and her family had abused the children. Cathy was only a year old when taken away, and so her abuse was minimal (according to what they usually see). She had some burn marks on her arm. It looked like someone had put a cigarette out on her arm a few times. Other than that, she seemed healthy. Come to find out Cathy wasn't with her birth mother's family much. Instead, she was left with a friend who took good care of her when she was in charge of her.

Cindy was almost three years old, and in pretty bad shape. Apparently, she had been put in a closet or small room, and she was ignored. She was mal-nourished so much so that her hair in the front of her head had fallen out. She was very thin. She wasn't potty trained, couldn't talk, had multiple bruises, fetal alcohol effect, and probably some attachment disorder. The caseworker requested that we call her current placement, and find out how she was doing. We proceeded to do that.

My husband made the call to Cindy's current placement. He was taking notes as the gentleman was giving him information regarding Cindy's condition. I was peeking over his shoulder to see what he was writing. As he wrote, I became very apprehensive about bringing her into our home. What did I know about caring for a child that wasn't mine—and was abused? I mean, big deal we went through 30 hours of training, but this was reality. I became very fearful about what we were contemplating doing. My parents were right; we were losing our minds!

When my husband got off the phone, out of my fearful heart, I informed him that I didn't think these two were the right two for us. He then reminded me that we had prayed long and hard that God would bring us the two children he had for our family. These were the two God brought us, and we would take them, and trust God. I knew he was right.

We called back the CPS worker and arranged to pick up Cathy the following week at the CPS office. Then we got to work. We had a bedroom to paint. We painted it yellow and purple, and had a Winnie-the-Pooh mural painted on the wall. It was so cute!

We needed to buy a crib, stroller, high chair, car seats, clothes, and all the other things that came with precious little girls. We hit a few yard sales, and found some toys that we thought would work great. We didn't know what size clothes the girls wore. Did the baby use a pacifier? What size diapers would we need? Was Cathy still on a bottle? It was a lot of fun preparing for their arrival, even though we had many questions that went unanswered.

We managed to get the bedroom decorated, and things in their proper place on time. The week went quickly, and finally the day that we had waited so long for was upon us. Matt and Ted were 16 and 14 at the time. We let them take the day off from school to go with us.

We arrived at the CPS office, and signed in. We were anxiously and nervously waiting for someone to come tell us what was going to happen next. While we were all sitting in the lobby, looking out the glass windows, we noticed an older gentleman get out of the car with a pudgy, beautiful little girl. She had a red barrette in her hair, and she was wearing a blue ruffle dress with white tennis shoes. She had the biggest, most beautiful, brown eyes we had ever seen.

The four of us commented on how precious that baby was and wouldn't it be amazing if that was Cathy? The older gentleman walked into the office with the baby and signed her in. You could have heard a pin drop. He began talking with the receptionist and of course, we were eavesdropping. We heard him state that he had transported the child, Cathy, for a visit with her parent. We were very excited. We told him we were there because we were to be her new placement as foster parents. He handed her to us, and allowed us to visit with her while we were waiting for the caseworker to show up.

Tom was holding Cathy on his lap. I was playing a game with her where I would take her shoe off and tickle her foot. She sat right there, belly laughing every time I tickled her—showing no fear whatsoever that she was with total strangers.

A few minutes later, three young women walked in together, signed in, and were sitting with us in the lobby. We found out that it was Cindy and Cathy's mom, and her two sisters.

Once CPS had taken the girls, the mom showed up and wanted them back. We had learned—in our thirty hours of class training—that all cases, no matter how difficult they may seem, or what the circumstances are, always start out with a case plan of reunification. They want to keep the children with their birth parents or birth families whenever it is possible.

We were new to this, and so it was a little awkward. We weren't sure if we should approach their birth mom and introduce ourselves. We ended up not talking to her that day, but it wasn't long before we had developed an amazing relationship with their birth mom that continues to this day.

A few minutes later, another individual walked in with another little girl. Her hair was a mess; she had on clothes that were too small and raggedy looking. She was running around like an animal that had been let out of its cage. It was Cindy. She went right to Tom and sat on his lap. We couldn't understand a word she said. She scared me. Honestly, I had never seen anything like it.

Tom was already in love with her, and the two of them were carrying on a conversation that only they could understand. My husband has such a special way with children. He is capable of loving and showing love to people that get overlooked. He amazes me. I have always told him that God called us to this ministry because of his ability to love.

We were left in the lobby to wait an hour for the visit with their birth mother to end, and then we would be free to leave with Cathy. We filled out the proper paperwork, and when the visit was over, we were ready to take Cathy home with us.

She came with one extra diaper, and the clothes on her back, so when I got home I had to hurry out and get her some clothes that fit. She was a little pudgier then I had imagined, and so I had to return some smaller outfits for larger ones. My boys were both skinny little things even as babies, and I was so excited to have a child with some fat cheeks to kiss.

The first day, as you can imagine, was busy, but fun. When bedtime came, I put her in her crib with a Winnie-the-Pooh blanket I had bought for her. She cuddled right up with it, lay down with her bottom up in the air, and went right to sleep. Throughout the night, I kept waking up to check on her. I was so worried that she would be scared being in a new environment, that I couldn't sleep—but she slept snug as a bug in a rug.

We spent the next week getting acquainted with Cathy. It was so much fun having a little one in the house again. The boys loved having her around. She adjusted quicker than I thought. I think it was because for the first year of her life, she was passed from home to home, whoever would watch her, and we were just another face among many.

She slept well, ate well, and clung to me. For quite a while, she didn't want to go to anyone else but me. So, she was a fixture on my hip. For the most part, she was an easy child to bring home.

She did have asthma, and I had never experienced a child with asthma. It was horrible. There were many nights I slept with her on my chest, afraid that she was going to stop breathing. I remember the doctor telling us to take her to an asthma specialist. When we called the specialist, we were informed that it would take a few months for her to be seen. I was disappointed that it would take that long, but it was understandable.

The very next day the phone rang, and it was the office of the asthma specialist. They said they had a cancellation, and asked if I could bring her in right away. You can bet I got in my car, and off we went. They were able to give her some medication that she began to take on a daily basis, and it cleared up the symptoms. It was such a blessing.

At visits with her birth mom, we noticed that there was no attachment between the two of them. It seemed they didn't know each other. Her birth mom spent the visit with Cindy, pretty much ignoring Cathy. We were informed that her mom gave birth to her, but never took care of her. She was passed from person to person. We believe though, that Cathy was able to bond with one of her caregivers—because she didn't have trouble bonding with us. Bonds are transferable, and we were thankful for that.

A week later, we drove back to the CPS office once again. The girls were having another visit with their birth mom. When it was over, we were able to take Cindy home.

The day she arrived, I was overwhelmed by her needs. I knew I was getting ready to lose it. I went over to my neighbor, who was a friend from church. I started crying, and once I started, I couldn't stop. I couldn't believe what I had just agreed to take on. I felt inadequate to meet this little girl's needs.

My friend and I sat together on the bench outside of her house. She prayed with me, and reminded me that we were called to take Cindy in, and that God would give us the wisdom and strength to help her. I realized she was right. I then thanked God for this amazing opportunity to pour my life into one so fragile. I blew my nose, wiped my eyes, and went back home. I then went shopping once again for some clothes that would fit her. She also came with nothing but the clothes on her back.

This was the beginning of a journey with Cindy. I am so privileged, now as I look back on her eleven years with us, that I was the one who got to watch God heal her mind and watch her transform into the beautiful young lady that she is today.

Before I share more about Cindy and the behaviors we had to deal with, I want to say that I believe that these children have great needs. If we can find the need, then meet the need, the behavior then can stop. There is a reason for the behavior that we cannot ignore. If we focus on the behavior, and not the reason behind it, we can miss the problem entirely. With that in mind, I will now share how we dealt with the needs of Cindy.

First, I found it strange that a child who was almost three years old went right to us, and showed no fear whatsoever. I noticed immediately that she called everyone *Mommy*. She called the doctor, *Mommy*, the cashier at the store *Mommy*—Daddy, brothers, grandparents, neighbors and strangers at church were all *Mommy* to her.

I began to explain to her that people had names. No matter where we were, she would run up to a total stranger, grab hold of them, and call them *Mommy*, and act like she knew them.

I would immediately grab her by her hand and pull her back away from the person and say, "Cindy, who is this? Do you know their name?" She would look at them. I would look at them. I would say, "I don't know their name, they are a stranger." I would then ask the person their name, and then tell Cindy, "This is Jane (or whomever). I am *Mommy*, and this is *Jane*. Do you know Jane? No, we don't know Jane." I would apologize to Jane for running up to her and grabbing her when we didn't know her (or him), whoever it may be at the time. And from there, I would take the time to explain to Cindy that there are strangers, and that we don't run up to strangers and grab hold of them.

Some people thought this was cute and harmless, especially at church, and they would embrace her when she ran up to them, even though they didn't know who she was. They might have thought I was unkind when I pulled her away from them. After all, she was in what you would call a *safe and loving environment*. I didn't care. I wanted to teach Cindy there are strangers, and not everyone is your friend. She needed to have physical boundaries herself, as well as respect others' boundaries. It took quite a while for her to stop calling everyone *Mommy*, and to realize those boundaries.

Cindy had a lot of night terrors. She probably had three a week. In the middle of the night, I would hear a bloodcurdling scream, and I would jump out of bed and run to her. I couldn't get there fast enough. She would be hysterical, and as I would reach for her, she would grab me, and cling to me—as if her life depended on it. I would hold her in my arms, rocking back and forth, until she calmed down, and then I rubbed her face until she fell asleep.

One of the things that I remember very clearly was the void look in her eyes. I remember rubbing her face while she looked up into mine, and I would tell her over and over again, that I loved her. I knew she had no clue what I was saying, and what love even was. During these times, I would also sing to her and pray over her. On many occasions, I not only prayed—I begged God to heal her mind from the abuse she had suffered. Many, many prayers were lifted up from me on behalf of this child. Wait until you hear the end of the story. My prayers were answered.

About four months after she came to live with us, a really neat thing happened. Once again, I was in the kitchen working when she came skipping towards me. She wrapped her tiny arms around my leg. I put my arm around her back and she looked up at me with those big brown eyes, and with a million dollar smile on her face. She said, "Mommy, I love you." I notice there was a light in her eyes that had not been there before. I knew for the first time in this precious child's life, she knew what love was. It was a moment to be remembered. PRICELESS!

Cindy was always checking to make sure I hadn't left the house, and that she could always find me close by. If she went out back to play, she would look in the back door every minute or so to make sure I hadn't gone anywhere. She had a fear of being abandoned.

I couldn't go to the bathroom and shut the door without the two girls sitting outside of the door screaming. They wouldn't play downstairs with their toys. They would bring their toys to wherever my feet were, set them down and they moved when I moved. For at least a year, the girls were all-consuming.

I can remember feeling like my husband, two boys, and I were passing each other, but not really seeing each other. I said to my husband more than once, "Are we okay? Are you okay?" He would assure me that he was. We all realized it was just a season, and eventually things would change. When we finally starting getting away on Saturday nights, we were so tired, we sat and yawned back and forth.

As for Matt and Ted, we were worried we weren't spending enough time with them either. We tried to spend some time alone with them, but they always assured us they were okay as well. They didn't want to exclude the girls in our times together, which was really sweet.

One night, I needed a break, and so I went to a concert with a friend. I would check in with my husband periodically to see how Cindy was doing. He informed me that she was an emotional wreck. He communicated to me that she kept walking around the house looking for me and saying, "Where'd Momma go?" She would sit on the couch, holding her favorite stuffed animal, crying off and on all evening. My husband assured her that I would return soon, but that offered little comfort to her. My husband said it was pathetic.

I felt like I had let her down, and caused her unnecessary stress by leaving. It bothered me so much that I thought about never going anywhere without her. But, that is not how you teach a child trust. What we decided to do was set a timer for ten minutes on the kitchen counter. I would tell Cindy that I was leaving, and that I would be back by the time the timer went off. I would leave the house, and I would come back ten minutes later. We did that several times, until she was comfortable with my ten-minute absence.

Then we moved the timer to 20 minutes, and so on. She learned that Mommy leaves; Mommy comes back. It worked very well. She would wait by the timer, and watch it move, and her anxiety eventually left—because she knew that when the timer went off, Mommy would be there.

P.S. Make sure you're there when the timer goes off.

Cindy was afraid of not getting food to eat. Before she came to live with us, she was locked in a closet or bedroom and wasn't fed regularly. When we fed her, she would shove the food into her mouth as fast as she could. She definitely was not okay with sharing her food. She would eat until she threw up if we let her.

If she saw someone with food, even a stranger at a store, she would run up to him or her, and try to take their food or she would ask them for a bite. I would have to pull her back, and once again explain that there are strangers and that we don't eat other people's food. We had plenty of food of our own.

We decided to leave boxes of food on the kitchen table, the kitchen counters, and everywhere in-between, for her to see at all times. If you were to come to our house you would have seen boxes of granola bars, Cheese-Its, fruit snacks, peanut butter crackers, and other items all out in the open.

When we gave her a snack or something to eat, she would begin to shove the food in her mouth as fast as she could swallow it. We stopped her, and explained to her there was more food where that came from. We would walk her around the kitchen, and show her all the boxes of food. We would then encourage her to slow down. Eventually, she realized that there was an abundance of food, and her fear of not being fed, left. It didn't happen overnight though.

She had a stuffed animal named Blue's Clues. One day, I was sitting downstairs on the couch, and I could hear her hitting and screaming at something and then a door slamming. A few minutes later, she came downstairs, and sat next to me with a satisfied look on her face.

I said, "Where is Blue's Clues?"

She replied, "He is bad. I spanked him, and put him in the closet."

I took her by the hand, and we walked upstairs together. I opened the hall closet door to find Blue's Clues lying on the floor of the closet.

I said, "Oh, poor Blue's Clues. Look how sad he is sitting in the closet all by himself."

She said, "He is bad, and that is where bad people go."

I said, "When you are bad, do Mommy and Daddy put you in the closet? No, we don't put you in the closet, and Blue's Clues doesn't want to be in the closet either."

She got him out, but when I turned my back, I heard her hitting him, and throwing him back in the closet. I would repeatedly take her by the hand and we would go rescue poor Blue's Clues from the closet. I would help her get him out, and tell her that we loved Blue's Clues, and didn't want to hurt him. This happened on many different occasions.

There were times, she would be playing with her dolls. She would scream at them, throw them across the room, hit them with a belt, and lock them in a closet or drawer. Afterward, she always had a satisfied look on her face.

I would pick up her baby, cradle it, and tell it how sorry I was that it had been hurt. She would watch me coddle it, and kiss its face, and then lay it down gently and lovingly.

Of course, I knew she was role-playing what had been done to her. I chose not to react, but to continue to model positive behavior from a mom to a child. Watching her struggle with this was very heartbreaking. It was a hard thing to watch, and believe me, it was a day to celebrate when that precious child stopped beating everything up, and instead turned into a loving, caring, nurturing child. FRONT ROW TO AMAZING!

She was also very afraid to come out of her room in the morning. I knew this was because she was locked in a room or closet before she came to live with us, and it was obvious to us that when she came out, she was punished. We never closed her door.

We explained to her that it was okay to come out of her room when she woke up in the morning. I would be waiting downstairs for her arrival. This didn't work, because she never came out of her room without me having to go get her.

We decided to try something else. Every evening, before she went to bed, Matt, Ted, Tom, and I would go up to her room with her. We would lay her in her bed and have her pretend to be sleeping. When she opened her eyes, we would say, "Cindy, are you awake? Then get up and go downstairs, because Mommy is waiting for you." She would jump out of bed, walk into the hallway, and then proceed to go downstairs where she was greeted by the four of us clapping and screaming, "Yeah, Cindy's awake!"

We practiced over and over, night after night, only to find her the next morning in her little blue and white princess pajamas, crouched in the corner, head between her legs, afraid to look up, and scared out of her mind to move. It was heartbreaking. We continued to encourage her to come out of her room on her own, by again practicing with her that evening, and every evening for many days.

One morning, I was in the kitchen getting the day started, and I looked up to see Cindy's big brown eyes peeking around the corner at me. I could see nothing but her eyes and the top of her little head as she was trying to see what I was doing, and if it was okay for her to be standing there. I yelled up, "Cindy, is that you?" No answer.

"Well, if those are Cindy's eyes I see, I sure hope she comes on down the stairs to see me." She then proceeded down the stairs, very slowly at first, making sure she wasn't going to be punished. When she made it to the bottom of the stairs, I greeted her with a big hug and kiss, and a breakfast made for a princess.

The very next morning I looked up to see her sitting on the top stair with a huge smile on her face. She had her little hands folded nicely on her lap. I could see in her eyes that she was proud of herself for sitting there, but also not sure if it was the right thing to do. She needed reassurance from me that her decision to come down on her own was the right one. With excitement in my voice, I said, "Oh my goodness, is that a precious little girl I see sitting on the stairs? You are so big and brave to come out of your room all by yourself. Get down here and see me." When she made it to me, we had a celebration of our own.

The next morning, she made it a few more steps farther down the stairs, and so on, until finally she felt comfortable coming all the way down to the kitchen without any encouragement.

It was one of the most amazing things to watch. This sweet little child was so afraid to just come out of her room in the morning. Something we all do, every day, without giving it a second thought. Watching this particular fear leave and be replaced by confidence was absolutely incredible!

Speaking of fear, Cindy had a tremendous amount of fear in many areas. Her fears were understandable when considering all she had been through in her first three years of life. Most children, as they grow, get to move about freely, touching and smelling things that are in their surroundings. Cindy didn't have the opportunity to do that. She was never introduced to the world around her. The consequences of that resulted in her being afraid of very normal situations.

She would scream bloody murder when she saw an ant—or any bug for that matter. One day, we were all sitting around the kitchen table, and the kids were all out back playing. We heard a horrifying scream. We thought someone had been hurt. Instead, Cindy saw an ant. She literally managed to get her whole body on the doorknob so that she was totally off the ground. It was an amazing sight to see—kind of funny when you think about it, and picture it. We had to pry her off the doorknob, and assure her that the little ant, the size of nothing, was not going to hurt her.

One evening, we went to a friend's house for dinner, and their daughter had a hamster. While the adults in the house were visiting, the children were all playing with the hamster. They were watching it while it was in its cage, as well as some of the older children were holding it. Cindy watched, but did not participate.

We got home, and put the kids to bed as usual. In the middle of the night, I heard another horrible scream. I ran to her bedside. She thought the hamster was in her bed, under her bed, in her closet, drawers, or somewhere in-between. She wasn't sure where it was, but she just knew it was somewhere in her room.

We took her room apart, so that I could show her that the hamster wasn't there—it was still at our friends' house. She would not believe me, or accept any comfort I gave. Instead, we spent the entire night lying in her bed together. She was tossing and turning, looking under her covers, and under her bed. She did not stay still, or fall back asleep for hours.

When we were playing, if she fell down or tripped, it was a horrific event in her life. She would scream like she was being attacked.

When Cindy first came to us, she couldn't talk, nor did she understand what we were saying to her. Things that a three-year-old should know, she didn't know. She had no idea what a spoon, or fork was, or how to use one for that matter. She ate with her hands, and it took quite a while to teach her how to use the proper eating utensils. She didn't know how to ask for a drink. She ran around grabbing things that she wanted, and she tried to talk with her hands instead of her mouth.

It seemed her teeth had been brushed very little, if at all. She had teeth that were rotting, and we spent quite a bit of time at the dentist getting her teeth healthy.

She couldn't obey simple instructions. I would ask her to get on my back so we could play horsey, and she had no idea what or where my back was. She was so pathetic.

We did what every parent does with his or her own children from day one. Unfortunately, Cindy didn't get it from day one, but thankfully, she did get it. We read books to her, played with her, and talked to her. I spent hours holding, rocking, and singing to her. Her favorite song was, *You are My Sunshine*.

It took a tremendous amount of time and energy to teach her the things she needed to learn.

I am happy to say that within a year of coming to live with us, she was talking to where we could understand her.

Shortly after Cindy arrived, we had her evaluated and placed in a developmental preschool. She was there because of her speech and developmental delays. She stayed in that particular preschool for two years. When Cindy was about to leave, her teacher asked if she could speak with me.

She said, "Do you know that Cindy is a miracle?"

I said, "Yes."

She stated that when she first met Cindy, she thought she should be placed in a mentally retarded classroom, but decided at that time she would see how things progressed with her. She certainly never thought Cindy would go to Kindergarten on time. And to kindergarten on time, she did go! She told us she didn't know how we had done it, but that Cindy truly was a miracle child.

I quickly let her know that we didn't do anything. We took this child in by faith, we prayed, loved, and worked tirelessly with Cindy, and that God is the one that was healing her, and would continue to heal her. We were just tools in the hand of God.

Since then, we have watched Cindy go on to the first, second, third grade, and on up—all on time, struggling some, but doing just fine.

On December 9, 2003, fourteen months after taking the girls into our home, we adopted them. We got up early in the morning, dressed them both in new outfits, and headed downtown to court. Tom's parents, my mother, and the six of us were there to witness this special day. We will never forget the judge saying, "As of this moment, your names are now......congratulations."

On the invitations to the celebration it read:

We've added to our family tree a stronger one to make

Two children from another plant have become our new namesake

Just as a limb is grafted from one tree to another

It alters and improves the plant making it, uniquely like no other.

Our family tree has been improved, adoption made this so.

For love, much more than bloodlines, makes us thrive and grow.

We chose to share our life and love and all the joys to come....

When you get a child, don't be scared. Don't be quick to label them. It is easy to find so many things wrong, because there probably are. But, it is amazing how quickly these children respond to a loving, structured, nurturing, predictable environment. Give them time to come to life!

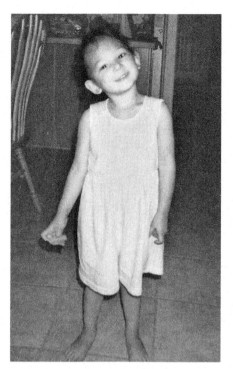
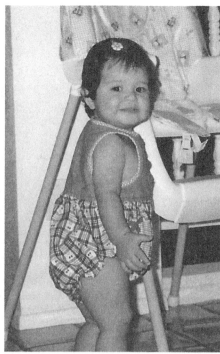

Cindy at age three (notice no hair due to malnutrition)
Cathy at age thirteen months
Below: Cindy and Cathy ages fourteen and twelve

Understanding the system

Foster parents, for the most part, operate in a gray area of the law. Their commitment and efforts are recognized as vital and essential to children in need. In court, their input is well-received due to their first-hand knowledge of the child's situation while in their home.

Foster parents have certain rights:

1. *To be treated with consideration and respect for the foster parent's personal dignity and privacy*

2. *To be included as a valued member of the team that provides services to the foster child*

3. *To receive support services that assist the foster parent to care for the child in the foster home, including open and timely responses from agency personnel*

4. *To be informed of all information regarding the child that will affect the foster home or family life during the care of the foster child*

5. *To contribute to the permanency plan for the child in the foster home*

6. *To have placement information kept confidential when it is necessary to protect the foster parent and the members of the foster parent's household*

7. *To be assisted in dealing with family loss and separation when a child leaves the foster home*

8. *To be informed of all agency policies and procedures that relate to the foster parent's role as a foster parent*

9. *To receive training that will enhance the foster parent's skills and ability to cope as a foster parent*

10. *To be able to receive services and reach personnel on a twenty-four-hour/ seven-days-a-week basis*

11. *To be granted a reasonable plan for respite from the role of foster parent*

12. *To confidentiality regarding issues that arise in the foster home*

13. *To not be discriminated against on the basis of religion, race, color, creed, sex, national origin, age, or physical handicap*

14. *To receive an evaluation on the foster parent's performance*

The more informed you can be on all the players involved in the system—and the roles they play—the better equipped you will be to handle what is in store. One of the greatest things you can do for yourself as a foster parent, is to become knowledgeable about how the system works, because ultimately you will have to use all the people in the system to your benefit to get all the services you will need.

A huge problem for foster parents is a misunderstanding about what everyone's role is in the system, as well as what everyone's role is in navigating the system.

You, as a foster parent, are going to walk into a system that has been in place for many years. You are thinking to yourself, I am entering a well-run machine and they should be able to help me navigate the system. You are going to have to be the one more active in exploring what everyone else's roles are, and what expectations they have for you in your new role as a foster parent. There may be times when you will have to force people to do their jobs. You can't do that if you are unclear on what their job entails.

It is very unfortunate that foster parents are left to figure out many answers on their own.

We have an overburdened system. Caseloads are way too high, and caseworkers can't always offer the assistance that foster parents may need.

Because the system is overburdened, this can affect the services provided—and the ability to get services in a timely manner: the types of services available change on a regular basis. Therapists change on a regular basis, which causes a lapse in services. This has a huge influence on the kids. When there is a disruption with ongoing, consistent, appropriate, services for these kids—it can be detrimental to the wellbeing of the child. The child may get use to one therapist, and then they leave. They get a new therapist, and they leave. Being bounced around from one therapist to another is never in the best interest of the child.

The large caseloads also impact the attorneys and GAL's. It affects their ability to appropriately advocate for their client. They struggle with being able to meet with all their clients, as well as to get services in place that will ultimately help make case plan changes. It can cause children to stay in the system longer than they should.

It is, however, important to understand that attorneys and guardians ad litem for children, have very clear obligations with regards to contact with the children they represent. Arizona law requires that they meet in person with the child before the first hearing (the preliminary protective hearing), if possible, or within fourteen (14) days after the hearing. Thereafter, it requires that they meet in person with the child before every substantive hearing. Substantive hearings include preliminary protective hearings, periodic review hearings, permanency hearings, hearings involving placement, visitation, or services, or any hearing to adjudicate dependency, guardianship, or termination. They may utilize appropriately trained support staff to assist them in this obligation.

I am going to take a few pages and talk about some statistics in the state of Arizona, go over some definitions that you will need to know and be aware of, as well as share how the system and hearings work.

Because we live in the state of Arizona, I will only share about the statistics in Arizona. As of March 31, 2013, there were 14,314 children in out-of-home-care. This number is 8% above the previous year. The number of CPS reports received by the Child Abuse Hotline has also increased to 44,322 projected for 2013. The majority of states have experienced a reduction in the number of children in foster care. Arizona has not. The numbers have continued to increase each year.

Every year, the state of Arizona receives thousands of calls to the child abuse hotline from people who are concerned about the safety of children. Investigators working for CPS are the ones who check out these concerns.

CPS investigates such family problems as:

1. *When children are being hurt by their parents*

2. *When children are not being protected by their parents*

3. *When children are left alone for a long time, or left in unsafe situations, (sometimes a parent has died or has been locked up in jail or prison)*

4. *When parents do not provide a safe home (sometimes because of serious mental health issues, alcohol or illegal drug use)*

5. *When parents do not provide critical medical care, or will not feed their children*

6. *When parents will not let their children live with them*

Most of the time, the CPS investigator is able to help the family with their problems, and keep children safe in their homes. But sometimes children must be removed from their home to be kept safe.

There is a lot of drug abuse in these families, as well as family dysfunction. It is a vicious cycle. The parents are usually doing to their kids what has been done to them—it is all they know.

This is where **foster care** comes in. Foster care is any placement for a child which is not in the home of a parent or legal guardian, and which may include a licensed foster home, group home or residential setting, a court ordered placement with a friend or relative, and an independent living setting. If CPS does not return the child back to his parents, they must ask the **Dependency Court** to agree to keep the child in foster care. They do this by giving a **Dependency Petition** to the court.

A **Dependency Petition** is a written report to the Court which tells why a child is not safe in the home, what CPS tried to do to help make things safe, why those things are not enough to keep the child safe at home, and why neither parent can care for the child. The petition must go to the judge within a few days of the child being moved from his or her home.

Once the court receives the Dependency Petition, the judge must read it right away, and decide if the child would be or would not be safe if living at home.

If the judge gets the dependency petition and decides that the home is not safe for the child, the judge will permit the child to stay in foster care until the first court hearing.

The first hearing is held a few days later, and is called a **Preliminary Protective Hearing or PPH.** All parents are invited to this hearing, but some may not come. Sometimes one or both parents cannot be found in time for the hearing. This hearing has to happen no more than 5 to 7 days from the child's removal from the home. .

At the PPH, the judge will ask the parents if they agree with CPS about where the child will live, and if they agree to get help for their problems. If the parents, CPS, and the judge agree, the child will be made a **ward of the court** — also called a **dependent child.** This usually means the child will stay in foster care while the parents work with CPS to solve their problems. The judge will continue to watch over what happens to and for the child.

If the parents do not go to the PPH, the judge will have everyone come back in a few weeks to hear from the parents. This is called the **Initial Dependency Hearing**. This hearing needs to take place no more than 21 days from the day the parents received the petition. Just like at a PPH, if the parents, CPS, and the judge agree, the child will remain a ward of the court (a dependent child) and the child will probably stay in foster care while the parents work with CPS to solve their problems.

If, however, the parents do not agree with CPS, and want their child back home, then there will be other hearings that happen within the next few months.

First, there will be a hearing so the judge can decide whether the child needs to be protected—even if the parents don't agree. This is called a **Dependency Adjudication Hearing.** At this hearing, the judge hears from the parents, CPS, and other witnesses who tell their side of the family story. It is the judge's job to listen to everyone, and decide what to do to keep the child safe. If the judge decides the home is safe, the judge will tell CPS to take the child back home—or the judge can decide that the parents need help before the child can go back home and be safe.

If the judge decides that the parents need help before they can have their child back home, there will be another hearing called a **Dependency Disposition Hearing**. At this hearing, the judge decides if the child should stay living where he or she is, or live somewhere else while the family works on getting help. Sometimes, both the Adjudication hearing and Disposition Hearing happen at the same time.

When the judge makes a decision to keep watch over the child, CPS tries to work together with the family to fix the family problems, and make the home safe for the child. Until the judge decides the home is safe, the child will live in foster care, and will get medical and dental care, go to school, and get other help (such as counseling). The judge continues to watch over the case, and everyone comes to court again for a **Report and Review Hearing**—which usually takes place every six months. Occasionally, the judge will bring everyone back together sooner to find out what is happening.

The judge will watch over the child through Report and Review Hearings as long as the child is in foster care, and sometimes even when a child goes back home, to make sure the child is still okay.

Every child in the system—regardless of age—has a right to attend their hearings, and speak directly to the judge. They can tell the judge how they are doing, if everything is okay, and what they (the child) think should happen. If for some reason they can't make the hearing, they can write a letter to the judge, or call their attorney and let them know what they want the judge to know. They should always be informed about when these hearings are going to take place.

The court wants, and encourages, foster parents to be involved. Court is a good place to have all their questions answered, and concerns expressed. It depends on the judge as to whether or not the foster parents are allowed to speak at a court hearing. Information is confidential, and they can close the proceedings, but most of them are open proceedings.

At any court hearing, the judge can return the child home if it is safe.

CPS and the parents have about one year to work together before the next big decision must be made. If the child is under the age of three, they have six months. After the time allotted, there will be a **Permanency Planning Hearing.** At this hearing, the judge again listens to the parents, CPS, and others talk about what everyone is doing to fix the family problems. The decision of what to do next is often very hard to make, so the judge will require CPS to suggest a good long-term plan to ensure the child can be healthy and safe. The court may change the case plan at this hearing, or may continue with reunification

The judge will decide how soon the child can go back home, which will depend on how well the parents are doing with solving their problems. Reasonable efforts must be made after placement to reunite the family. The judge will consider the parents' compliance with services such as: visitation, counseling, psychological evaluations, parent aid services, respite services, and counseling. If the judge decides it is not safe for the child to go back home, the judge may tell CPS to find another permanent home for the child. This could be living with relatives or friends permanently, or being adopted by another family.

Generally, CPS is supposed to ask for an order from the court to change physical custody of the child from a foster home to a relative. The relative will need to have a background check, criminal background check, home study, and a check of the CPS Central Registry to see if there are any prior referrals. If everyone agrees on moving the child to a relative, usually the judge just signs off on the order.

If there are several siblings in different homes, and there is a family willing to take all siblings and keep them together, they may move them all from their current foster home to a new one. Children are in the legal custody of DES. Foster parents are licensed with DES, so they can be moved from foster home to foster home without a court order. Once you are identified as an adoptive home, CPS cannot move the child without a court order. Unfortunately, this happens far too often.

Sometimes, a child will stay in foster care until they are at least 18 years old.

Depending on the decision of the judge, other hearings may be needed. If the judge decides that a child should be adopted by another family, there must first be a court hearing to decide whether the parents will no longer be able to make decisions about where the child will live and how to take care of the child. The judge will consider and look at the services DES offered the parents. This is called a **Termination of Parental Rights (TPR) Hearing.** Termination of parent/child relations is a serious matter. The state agency has a duty to make all reasonable efforts to preserve the family relationship, rather than use its power to snatch away a child. The natural parent also has to make a good faith effort to unite the family.

Arizona law provides the following specific grounds for the termination of parental rights:

(1) Abandonment

(2) Neglect or willful abuse

(3) Mental illness, mental deficiency, or substance abuse

(4) Felony conviction of a parent

(5) Parental relinquishment of rights or consent to adoption

(6) Failure to establish paternity following notice required or notice of claim of paternity

(7) Length of time in out-of-home placement

(8) Unknown identity of parent for three months

(9) Termination of parental rights in preceding two years for same cause

(10) Return of child to parent, and subsequent removal within 18 months

If the judge does end the parents' rights, it is CPS' job to make sure the child finds a good, forever, adoptive family. Many times, the child is adopted by a relative, or his or her foster parent. There are many steps to a child being adopted; however, the final step is the **Adoption Hearing** where the judge decides that the child will be placed with the adoptive family forever. At this hearing, the judge must ask a child—who is age 12 or older—whether they want to be adopted by the family. If the judge and the child agree, then the adoption is approved.

When an adoption is approved, the judge and CPS are no longer involved with the child and the child's adoptive family.

Sometimes, adoption is not what's best or possible for a child. In that case, the judge may decide that a child should permanently live with a relative, a family friend, or the child's foster family until the child is at least 18 years old. This would require another type of hearing called a **Guardianship Hearing**. If the judge agrees to a guardianship, then the family the child is with will make all the decisions for the child—even though the rights of the child's birth parents have not ended. The child has to be in the custody of the prospective permanent guardian for at least nine months as a dependent child, and reasonable efforts to reunite parent and child have to have been made. Adoption is remote, and severance would not benefit the child. Guardianship takes away the birth/adoptive parent's legal custody, but does not terminate parents' rights. If everyone agrees, the child could continue to have contact with the birth parents even after the guardianship is approved. Report and Review hearings are required after the first year of guardianship.

When the child cannot go back home, and adoption or guardianship are not possible, the child might stay in foster care until he is at least 18 years old. In this case, the judge may agree to a case plan called, **Alternative Planned Permanent Living Arrangement**, where the child continues to go to school, get services and skill training to help learn what they need to know about being an adult, before leaving foster care.

By law, a child becomes an adult when they reach the age of 18. At that time, the judge cannot make any more decisions about the young adult in foster care. But, these young adults can choose to stay in foster care to receive help with services and life decisions until they are 21, or they can choose to leave foster care when they turn 18 (or older).

If a young adult leaves foster care, and then decides that he or she really does need the help and support that CPS can provide, they can return to CPS for help until they are 21. Former foster children who want to return for help from CPS through the independent living program, must contact CPS directly. The court is no longer involved.

After a child is safe at home, in an adoptive home, in a guardian's home, or has turned 18, the Dependency case is closed, and no more court hearings are held.

What do Attorneys do? Attorneys or lawyers are specially trained people who give advice and represent clients, such as parents and children in dependency court. The attorney's job is always to tell the judge what their client wants, and why the judge should agree with their client. The attorney should explain the entire court process to the child (if old enough), tell the child when hearings are set, what could happen at the hearing, and answer any questions the child may have about what is going on in the case.

What is a GAL? A GAL is also known as a *Guardian Ad Litem*. A GAL's job is to tell the judge what the GAL believes is best for the child. To do that, the GAL should meet with the foster parent and child to better understand the needs of the child. They should meet prior to any substantive hearings—which are Preliminary Protective Hearings, Report and Reviews, as well as trials. They will need to know any problems and concerns that you as the foster parent see. The GAL will look at the family's case record, and also do their own investigation to help decide what would be best for the child.

Because an attorney's job is to represent what the child wants, an attorney is usually appointed for a child who is old enough to be able to say what they want. For young children, a GAL is usually appointed to tell the judge what is best for the child. However, an older child may have an attorney to tell the judge what the child wants and a GAL to tell the judge what the GAL thinks is best for the child.

The foster child's CPS caseworker has the information on the GAL assigned to his case. You can get the phone number and other information regarding the GAL directly from them.

Who are CASAS and what does a CASA do? Court Appointed Special Advocates (CASAs) are volunteers who are specially trained to "advocate" for the child, and advocate for everything the child needs in order to be safe and healthy. Not all children have a CASA. If a child is appointed a CASA, the CASA will meet with the child often, spend time getting to know them, do their own investigation, look at the records, attend all meeting and court hearings, and write a report which goes directly to the judge before each court hearing. The judge will listen very carefully to the CASA's opinions and recommendations.

Case Plan: A written report that tells about the problems in the family (the reasons for court involvement), what is needed to help fix those problems, what each person must do to fix the problems, and when those things should be done.

Most case plans start out with a case plan for reunification. There can be some confusion on the part of the foster parent as to why the case plan isn't changing as quickly as they think it should. That is because there is a lack of understanding of the law. The child may also get a judge assigned to their case that believes very strongly in protecting parental rights.

There are certain types of cases where allegations regarding the parents are severe enough to have the option to immediately implement a case plan of severance.

What does the Foster Care Review Board do? The Foster Care Review Board (FCRB) is a group of people who look at what is going on with dependent children who are placed out of their parents' homes. These people do not work for CPS, but are asked by judges to review cases of children in foster care at least once every six months. Parents, CPS, and other interested people attend these reviews to tell them how things are going, and what needs to happen next. The FCRB writes a report to the judge telling the judge what they think is happening, and should happen, in the case.

The FCRB wants to hear from all children in foster care. The foster family should receive a green notice inviting them to a FCRB review about one to two weeks before your case is to be reviewed.

All foster parents should attend the review, and if possible, bring the foster children in their care with them. This is the *first bite* at the apple to explain how the child is doing, and to express your opinion. If for some reason you cannot attend, you can e-mail, fax, or call in to leave a message for the Board before the review date. In some counties, you may participate by conference call.

Appeal: The legal process by which a *party* to a dependency asks a higher court (the Court of Appeals) to review a decision of the dependency court judge—about ordering or dismissing a dependency, where the child lives, and certain other issues. If a party disagrees with the judge's decision, they must file an appeal within 15 days of the date the decision was made. The appeal can take up to one year to complete. Do not proceed with an adoption until the appeal has been resolved.

Child Protective Services (CPS) Case Manager: A specially trained person who is responsible for investigating problems that are reported about a family situation, or may be responsible for getting services to help a family resolve its problems. The case manager will check on children in foster care, and the other family members, to see how everyone is doing, and write a report to the court about the progress the child and family are making before each hearing.

Ongoing Licensing worker: Initially, your licensing worker will help you assess your family, and come to a decision as to whether or not foster care is right for you. If it is, it is their job to get you through licensing. Once you have your foster care license, your licensing worker will monitor and support you and your family and give you direction, make sure your house stays to regulation, and you are following all rules, do your quarterly inspections and licensing renewal, as well as complete any licensing investigations. They are your family's worker, listening to your needs, and making sure there isn't a negative impact on your own family. It is their job to also make sure the needs of the foster child are appropriately being met in your house.

Parent aid: You may, or may not, come in contact with a parent aid. They may be available to transport a child to a visit with their parent, as well as supervise a visit. They also meet with the biological parents individually, and spend some time teaching them parenting skills, and giving them direction for the future.

CFT: or Child and Family Team – Where the mental health provider has a meeting with all involved parties to discuss services available to get help for the child.

A message from William Owsley, Dependency Division Chief in the office of the Legal Advocate:

Being a foster parent will be one of the most difficult, and most reward-ing things you will ever do in your life. There will be times when you'll feel ignored and undervalued by those in the system. Even children themselves seldom offer thanks. Don't be discouraged. Just know how important you are to this child. Know that you are uniquely situated to have the most significant impact on their life. You will impact who they are, the relationships that they have with their families and future spouses, their own children and their fu-ture successes. The impact will last forever. Provide them with the tools to be successful. Give them unconditional love. Nothing you do is wasted. Nothing.

Children are the living messages we send to a time we will not see.

— Neil Postman, *The disappearance of Childhood* (introduction), 1982.

Mike and Joy

Cindy and Cathy had been living with us for a year when I received a call from the parent aid that had worked with the girls. She told me about a five-year-old little boy that was on her caseload. She informed me that he was in a shelter, and had been there for three months. She also informed me that after every visit with his parents, he cried because he didn't want to go back to the shelter.

She said that as far as she knew, he didn't have any behavioral issues, and she thought he would fit beautifully in our home. She thought it would be an easy case, and he probably would only be with us for about a year—and she wondered if we would be interested in fostering him. I told her, "No." I certainly didn't want a boy, and a five-year-old one at that.

About a month later, she called again regarding the same little boy. I mentioned it to my husband, but I still wasn't interested.

The next month we adopted Cindy and Cathy, and Christmas was quickly approaching. I couldn't get the little boy in the shelter out of my mind. I kept thinking about how he would spend Christmas in a shelter, when we had a perfectly good room for him here at the house.

Of course, it wasn't long until the parent aid called again, letting me know he was still stuck in a shelter—and hating it. She once again asked if we would consider placing him into our home.

Tom was working at home at the time, and so we were sitting in the kitchen having lunch together. For some reason the boys were there too. I said, "You know that little boy in the shelter? Maybe we should consider bringing him in here for a year." Matt and Ted wanted to know what little boy I was speaking of. Tom's response shocked me.

He replied, "I have been waiting for the Holy Spirit to speak to your heart and let you know he should come live with us."

I said, "Why didn't you just tell me that?" But you see, Tom and I never tried to convince each other to bring a child into our home. We knew if it was what we were supposed to do, we would both know it individually.

Matt and Ted also chimed in. They couldn't believe we had been asked to foster a child, and we had turned them down. They wanted us to go get him immediately. I felt like the odd man out.

I called the CPS caseworker, and set up a time to go pick him up. In the meantime, we went Christmas shopping for a child we had never met. It was three days before Christmas when we walked into the shelter—to see a little boy in a sweat suit four sizes too big, staring up at us with big brown eyes, and an adorable smile on his face. I knew then that we were taking him home. His name was Mike.

After we got him home, the caseworker came to our house with all the necessary paperwork. She informed us at that time that he had a baby sister that was also in a shelter, and they wanted to keep the siblings together. Would we consider taking her in too? We had the room, but four kids under the age of five, seemed like a lot. I was helping my husband in the office at the time. He told me he could hire someone to work part-time, and we could also hire a housekeeper so that I could devote all my attention to the children.

Why are children in the system? We all know it is mostly because of neglect and abuse. I don't know what I was thinking. When I heard Mike had a seven-month-old sister, I was picturing a child that was crawling, sitting up, giggling, and getting ready to walk in the next few months. That is not what we received.

It was two days before Christmas, and I was sitting across the street talking to a neighbor on her swing when the car pulled up. I saw the caseworker get out of the car, and she was holding a baby like you would hold a newborn. I wondered why that was. I thought I was getting a child that would rest on my hip. I followed them across the street, and peeked at a tiny little bundle of nothing. She wore a beanie that covered her very tiny head. She was sucking her fingers, and was wrapped tightly in a blanket. When we took the blanket off, she had on a boy's blue sleeper.

I asked her caseworker when she had last eaten…she had no idea. She had no extra diapers—literally, nothing but the blanket she was wrapped in, and the sleeper she was wearing. I asked if they were sure she was seven months old. They replied that she was, even though she was barely 10 pounds. We filled out the necessary paperwork, and they left. I sobbed!

I couldn't believe what we had decided to do, and two days before Christmas. What in the world were we thinking? Once again, I couldn't stop crying. I called a good friend. She prayed with me, and then got in her car with her daughter and came to our house. Her daughter watched the other kids while we ran to the store for food, bottles, diapers, and everything else that we would need to care for this child. It was indeed overwhelming.

While I was away getting the supplies I needed for Joy, my parents stopped in to meet our newest addition, Mike. They had no idea we had taken not only Mike, but baby Joy. I think they were in shock. That's always a fun thing to do, shock the parents. Just make sure their heart is good before you pull out the shock factor.

It didn't take long for my parents to love both new children. My dad spent Christmas morning holding Joy on his lap, while the other children opened their presents. He was instantly hooked. From that day forward, Joy had Grandpa wrapped around her itty-bitty tiny finger!

It was fun to watch Mike open his presents. We bought him his first bike, and a huge black bear stuffed animal. He also got some holsters and guns to play with. I remember him being so happy, because he had never had a bike before. It was sweet to watch.

The kids got along from day one. There didn't seem to be any jealousy between the four of them. They became an instant family, playing together, and caring about each other early on—which made it easier on us.

It didn't take more than an hour with Joy to realize that her abuse was severe. She threw up constantly. Every time I took her to the doctor, he would check her weight. She was gaining, and so he wasn't too concerned about her throwing up. He figured some of the food was staying in her stomach. At a year and a half, she was still in six-month clothes, but she was growing.

At seven months, she couldn't sit up, roll over, laugh, or cry. She just looked at us with no emotion whatsoever. It was unlike anything I had ever seen. She had no personality of her own. She lay perfectly still, always sucking her fingers, and she just looked around—never making a peep.

I always thought that babies were the easiest of foster children to take into your home. They couldn't sass you, spit on you, or make your life too difficult with their behavior. I have learned that babies can be just as hard as older children, just in a different way.

Because Joy had not been held, fed, or loved, her coloring did not look healthy. She also had no hair, but the hair directly on top of her head—and it stuck straight up. One day, a family member was visiting. I had a picture of Joy on my refrigerator, and she commented that she was glad there was such a thing as makeup because Joy was certainly going to need to use it.

Another time, while at church, a friend came up and commented on how homely Joy was.

I couldn't believe it. This child was lifeless because of her abuse. I don't care if she was a foster child and not my own flesh and blood. I felt those comments were rude and hurtful.

Once Joy was fed, loved, and nurtured, her color came in and she was a beautiful little girl!

I also remember sitting in church holding Joy on my shoulder while she slept. Someone came up to me and said, "Why would you take in more children?" I didn't respond—because I don't think people that say things like that deserve a response. When they left, I remember I got tears in my eyes as I was sitting there. However, I did think to myself, holding that precious infant to my breast, "Because they are safe and loved now. As long as they are with me, they won't be hurt. That's why."

Over the next few years, we watched Joy improve. She finally made it on the growth chart, although even to this day she is still very small. She didn't cry until she was 11 months old. When a child is born, they cry which expresses a need. The caregiver meets the need, which then stops the crying. If a child cries and the need doesn't get met—they eventually stop crying.

I would go into her room in the morning, or after a nap, and I would find Joy just lying there, sucking her fingers, not making a sound. I would try to get her to respond to me, but she didn't do anything except give me a blank stare. It was so very sad!

She also failed to laugh until she was almost 11 months old, and when she did laugh, it was nothing more than a small chuckle. We were all impressed though.

She didn't walk until she was a year and a half.

When she was four years old, her sister fell on her and it broke her leg. She is very fragile to this day, and we call her our *Little Peanut*.

In the world of foster care and adoption, many things will tug at your heart and be very difficult for you. I can remember taking her to the doctor for the first time. Remember she couldn't sit up, roll over, and she didn't cry. She was a poor, pathetic little life. The doctor wasn't sure if she was failure to thrive, or if her situation was all environmental. I took her home, and began to feed and love her. I remember the day I took her back to the doctor, and she was actually on the very bottom of the growth chart. The doctor and I were high-fiving each other. It was a proud moment.

As I was putting Joy in her car seat, I began to cry, and I cried all the way home. I was so scared that she would be returned to her birth parents, and that they would starve her again. When I got home, my husband asked me what was wrong. I shared with him that I couldn't stand the thought of having someone hurt her again. What if she was returned home, and they didn't care for her? He said, "Well, we knew there would be pain involved when taking in these kids." He reminded me that she was not ours, and that we would trust God with the outcome—easier said than done, that's for sure.

They don't belong to us, and it can be emotionally difficult, because you grow to love them, and the goal is to give them back to a situation that may be less than perfect. Most foster parents realize they can give the child in their care better care, and more opportunities, than they would get if returned to their birth parents. Staying focused on the fact that they are *not ours* can be difficult. I began to pray that day, that if Joy's parents weren't going to feed her and care for her, that God would not allow her to be returned to them. I not only prayed, if I remember correctly—I begged.

When she was about a year and a half, she found her lungs, and realized that if she screamed—we came running. She cried for the next year. She wanted to be held nonstop. I even took her to the doctor to see if something was physically wrong with her. I wondered if she was in pain, and that was why she cried all the time. The doctor assured me she wasn't crying because of a physical aliment. He felt that she was very emotionally delayed, and she had just realized she could have her needs met, and so she let her need to be held known very loudly. It was a rough time.

To this day, the housekeeper still talks about Joy screaming all the time. I would walk into a room and find the housekeeper rocking Joy, because she was crying and I hadn't gotten right to her. It was precious. It wasn't long, and Joy had everyone wrapped around her finger. Everyone that knows Joy, will say, "There is something special about that child." And indeed there is.

As she grew, we noticed her speech was delayed. We had her evaluated, and she qualified for speech therapy. She began attending a developmental preschool to help with that. We wondered if she would ever be able to utter a complete sentence. She did, but she was about three years old.

She didn't swim until she was nine years old, and she didn't ride a bike until she was eight. Part of the problem with those things, is because she is very fearful to try new things. She doesn't have a lot of confidence.

It took a year or two of sitting in the same dental chair before she would open her mouth. Now, she has to have the same hygienist clean her teeth at every visit. I don't know what we will do if the hygienist quits. We laugh, because she asks us if we think she needs braces. We say it doesn't matter if you need them or not. We know she would never open her mouth for the orthodontist.

For a long time, she had difficulty with change. When I changed the sheets on her bed, I would have to replace them with the same color sheet and pillowcase. If it was different, she would freak out. She has gotten over that now, thank goodness.

She struggles in school. She is delayed in math, and she has a hard time putting words together. She also has a hard time reading. One of the biggest problems is her memory. She can't remember from one day to the next what she has already learned.

Socially and emotionally, she is very young. We figure she is about two years behind schedule. We thought once you took a baby, loved, and nurtured that baby, they would be "normal" and healthy. That is not necessarily the case. When a baby has had little to no interaction with a human, is not fed, and left to lie in a bed—it affects their brain development. It is worse than a drug baby.

Let's get back to Mike, Joy's older brother. Mike was almost five when he moved in, and to be honest it was difficult from day one.

We will get to the behaviors he exhibited in a minute, but first, I'll talk about what happened in visits with his parents. His parents were very upset, which is understandable—that he was in the care of the state. We tried to reach out to them, and show them that we had nothing against them, and were hoping and praying that they would get their children back—if they made the necessary changes in their lives and home.

When we took these children, we had no intention of adopting them. We were told that it was a simple case, and it should only last a year. Three years later, we would be faced with the decision of adoption.

In the beginning, they took Mike to his parent's apartment for the visit. A lot of the time, his dad wouldn't even get out of bed to spend his one-hour-a-week with him. He said he would spend time with him when he got him back. His mom was always there.

Children are smart. Mike figured out relatively quick that his parents hated us. At his weekly visits, the parents drilled him concerning life at our house. They spent most of their time talking about why they hated us, and Mike was a captivating audience.

In the beginning, we sent pictures of Mike with him on a visit with his parents, so his parents could see what kinds of things he was doing. Our intention was to let the parents see that he was safe, and having a good time. The pictures showed him riding a skateboard with our sons, as well as some fun at the lake. The pictures had the opposite effect of what we were trying to accomplish. We were informed not to send any more pictures, because the parents wouldn't stop questioning Mike. We were told it made Mike very uncomfortable.

When the kids come into our home, we tell them our name and they are free to call us whatever they are comfortable with (Mom, Dad, Jill, or Tom). Every child that could talk entered our house calling us Mom and Dad immediately, or soon after they arrived. I still think that is weird, especially with the older kids.

I remember when Mike asked if he could call us Mom and Dad. I think he wanted to do that, because the other children in the home all called us Mom and Dad, and he wanted to do the same. I said "Sure." I explained that we would be his mom and dad in this house. I explained that it was all right to have two moms and two dads. That was more people for you to love, and to love you back.

Mike went to a visit, and when referring to my husband, he called him *Dad*. Mike's dad flipped out. He screamed at Mike, and told him Tom was not his dad. He had *one dad,* and he better never call Tom *Dad* again. Mike came home from this particular visit, and told Tom he was not his dad, and he was going to call him *Tom* from that day forward. We said, "Okay." Within ten minutes, he had forgotten his promise to call Tom, *Tom,* and was instead calling him *Dad* once again. He was trying very hard to please his biological father. After every visit, he would come home in turmoil, and he was always very shaken up. It would cause him to act out, and wet his pants for at least three days.

There is such a thing as loyalty. If all the adults involved (Child Protective Service caseworker, GAL, parents, foster parents, parent aids, etc.) can work together with the best interest of the child in mind, than the child is free to enjoy life without trying to fix and maintain relationships.

Mike loved his parents, and didn't want to upset them. He wanted them to know from the get-go, that he was on their side. He was loyal to them. If he liked living with us, then it would upset his parents, and he didn't want to do that. He began making up lies about us. When there is an accusation against a foster parent, no matter what that accusation is, Child Protective Service has to look into it. We would get a call about every week.

Mike once told his parents that we put Joy in the fireplace. Our caseworker loved us, and knew the accusations were not true, but she still had to call and ask. This particular call just cracked us up.

We asked Mike if he told his parents we put Joy in the fireplace, and he responded that yes, he did.

So, I said, "When do I put Joy in the fireplace? Is it when I feed her, or put her to bed?" He said nothing, so then I talked to him about lying. I explained that if someone decided to believe his lies, he might be taken away and put back in the shelter, and we didn't want that to happen. It was very important that he tell the truth at all times.

Mike was doing what any child would do. He was being loyal to his parents. When he would go to visits and tell his parents how *terrible* we were, his parents would coddle him, feel sorry for him, and he in turn felt like he was on their side. We don't want kids to have to pick sides. It would be wonderful if all the team players could work together for the benefit of the child. However, this is not always possible. It then makes it very difficult for the child to live a life free from stress.

When Joy was learning to stand up, she stood while taking her bath. I was sitting on the toilet seat right beside her, watching her. She managed to slip and hit her face on the side of the tub. I tried to grab her in time, but didn't quite make it. It gave her a black eye. *Oh my goodness*! You would have thought I killed her. We wrote an incident report, but there were still the parents' accusations of us abusing her that had to be dealt with.

They complained that we gave Joy too much apple juice. They didn't like the school we enrolled Mike in. They didn't want Mike and Joy going to church with us. The complaints went on and on. It was exhausting.

For a while, I was transporting the kids to visits every week. One week, I dropped the kids off at the library for a visit, and as I was walking back to my car I ran into Joy's mom and their dad (Joy and Mike had the same dad, different moms). They saw me, and their dad started to come at me like he was going to hit me. I continued to walk to my car, never slowing down or stopping. I don't remember what words were exchanged. I know they weren't nice on his part. I remember that I looked right at him, and told him he wasn't going to bully me. I never stopped, I continued walking to the car, got in, and went home, but I was shaking.

I called the kids' caseworker, and told her that I didn't want to be put in that position again. They knew how mad the dad was, and how unpredictable he could be. From then on, I dropped the kids off a block from the meeting place, and the parent aid took them the remaining block to the visit. That way, I didn't have to run into their dad again.

Every parent is entitled to reasonable visitations with their child—unless the court determines that visitation would seriously endanger the child's physical, mental, moral, or emotional health. Eventually, the parent aid had enough, and she felt that the visits between Mike and his dad were not beneficial. They had Mike meet with a psychologist, and they determined that the visits moving forward would just be between Mike and his mom. His dad was not happy.

Another situation we ran into with visits: Mike's mom would always bring him a toy. He would bring the toy home. He was very protective of the toy, because it was from his mom—which is totally understandable. When he left the toy on the floor, and another child would pick it up, Mike would attack them. It was horrible, and it happened every week. We couldn't stop it, and he wouldn't put the toy away in his room. I finally told the parent aid that the toys Mike's mom bought him, needed to stay at visits. He could play with them there with her. If the toy came home with him, I would put it in a bag in the closet, for Mike to have at a later time.

Visits can be very hard, but they are also very important. It is easy for foster parents to get frustrated because of all the work visits can create. The child may come home and act out, and usually the acting out lasts for a few days. You will go through the acting out process every week. The parents don't always show up, and you are left with the disappointed child to deal with. The parents promise them things that can't happen, and you know it can't happen. When it doesn't, you again are left to deal with the disappointed child. It goes on and on.

You, as a foster parent, have to be ready to deal with the ups and downs of visits. The parents have a right to see their child, and your job is to encourage

the visit between the biological parents and the child. This can be very difficult, but necessary.

Before I get into our time with Mike, I will explain how the adoption of
Joy and Mike came to be. If you remember, this was supposed to be an easy
case, and we didn't take them with any thought of adoption. I want to be very
honest here, even if it doesn't sound *right*. It is what it is. I want our experiences to hopefully help someone else, and if I am not honest, than I am cheating
us all out of the possibility of learning from one another.

Mike and Joy's case ended up being a rather difficult case. Take note of
this. When a case comes into Child Protective Services, they do not know what
is going to happen. Parents that have been uninvolved suddenly show up. Family members come forward as well. They really cannot predict how the case
will go. You need to know that before getting into this.

Mike's dad, John, lived with Mike's mom, Jane. Jane was mentally dis-
abled, and so she got SSI from the state. John didn't like to work, he liked to
play video games, and so he lived off the kindness of others and off Jane's SSI.
They had Mike together, but then John met Joy's mom, Kim. She was also
getting assistance. She had two other children from a previous relationship,
and soon she was pregnant with Joy. John decided he wanted to be with Kim,
but Jane didn't want to leave John. So, they came up with a plan to all live
together. That way, John still didn't have to work, and now he had two girls to
support his video game habit. Did you keep up?

John was caught abusing Kim's two children from another relationship.
All of the children were removed from the home because Kim and Jane would
not leave John. Therefore, it was a *failure to protect* issue. The state was hoping the girls would eventually leave John. They did everything the state asked
them to do, but wouldn't leave John, and John did nothing the state required
him to do to get his children back. Therefore, there was a safety issue. The
state decided the kids could not be returned.

It took two years for the state to make that decision. They wanted to give
Kim and Jane every chance to leave John. After two years, all of their rights
were terminated. They then appealed the case, which took another year.

When parental rights are terminated, they have what they call a *final visit* between the parent and child. On Mike's final visit, his dad was not invited. He was to visit with his mom and grandma. When I arrived there, I saw John and Kim hanging around outside. I realized they had been informed of the visit from Jane, and they were probably planning to make things difficult for CPS. We didn't want the visit to be any worse for Mike then it had to be.

It was a potentially dangerous situation. I was alone in the car, and couldn't be confronted by John. I knew he was angry at the system, and could possibly try to take Mike from me. I called CPS, and told them I wasn't going to pick him up after his visit. For my safety, we agreed to meet across town in an undisclosed area. CPS drove him to me, only after making sure they weren't being followed.

Child Protective Services informed us that Joy and Mike were going to be placed up for adoption. They told us they had no family that was a suitable placement (that wasn't true, and I will get to that later in the chapter). The kids had been living with us for three years, and CPS wanted to know if we would adopt them.

It was now decision time. We had Joy since she was an infant, and had bonded with her. We were the only parents and family she had ever known. We loved her, and were very willing to adopt her and become her forever family.

Mike came at age five, and was difficult from day one. We loved him, but I did not want to adopt him, because the last three years of my life with him were more than difficult (being honest, remember).

The problem we faced was that CPS wanted to keep the children together. I told Tom, Matt, and Ted that I didn't want to adopt Mike, and if that meant losing Joy, then I was willing to take that chance. Maybe they would let us keep Joy, since we had her from the beginning—and they would find another home for Mike. The three of them disagreed with me.

They knew Mike was difficult, but they felt that Mike belonged with us, because he had been here so long. They wanted him to be in a Christian home, and with his sister. And for goodness sake, he had *nowhere else to go*. We did love and care for him, I just didn't want to raise him. So, instead of asking CPS if we could adopt only Joy, we decided to tell them we would adopt both of them. That is how the adoption came to be.

I did agree with the three of them that it would be in the best interest of Mike to stay with us. So, I decided I would commit myself to being his parent, and being the best parent I could be for him.

On adoption day, we once again got the kids new outfits, got up early, and headed off to the courthouse. Our mothers were there, along with Mike's grandmother and a few of our friends. It was a very special day. We celebrated a few days later with all our family and friends.

In the next few pages, I will explain some of the problems in detail that we had with Mike, so you can better understand the rest of the story.

When Mike came to live with us, we noticed that he broke everything. He would break his toys and everyone else's. He broke the outside grill, the cup holders in the car, the door handle, and the light switch in his bathroom. One night, when he was doing dishes, he managed to break the faucet at the kitchen sink. I mean break, like break in two. We never did figure out how he pulled that one off. He broke anything he could get his hands on. That behavior never stopped. It got to a point that if we saw him with someone else's things, we would make him give it back immediately, knowing that in a few minutes it would be in pieces.

He had a knack for spitting in the other kids' faces. One time, the kids were hooked into their car seats, and for no reason Mike leaned over and hocked a loogie in Cindy's face. He did this on multiple occasions. That behavior took quite a while to stop. When he was about 11, he spit once again in Cindy's face. I was furious. We had dealt with this issue on so many occasions, I was done talking with him about it.

I told him the next time he spit in someone's face—I was going to spit in his. I didn't know what else to say, I don't even know if I would have gone through with it. I just know I had had enough. I am fortunate that my threat seemed to solve the problem. That was the last time he spit on someone.

He would constantly *accidentally* hit people in the face. This was a problem. He would have a ball in the pool, and would *accidentally* manage to hit his sister in the face with it, and she wasn't even in the pool. If he had a bat, a ball, anything that could fly through the air, it always ended up in someone's face. It was more than frustrating. He always said it wasn't on purpose, but we knew something was wrong. This behavior never stopped. He even got detention a few times at school for *accidentally* hitting someone in the face with a ball.

From day one, Mike was plainly defiant. He tore wallpaper off the walls, and he rubbed his snot on the walls. He would act like he didn't hear us, and he would turn around and do the opposite of what he had been asked to do. He wouldn't obey the simplest of rules—like stay in your bedroom at bedtime. If his mouth was open, he was usually telling a lie. Remember: this is the child I was told had no behavioral issues.

Some of these behaviors are normal; what made them hard was his age, and that he never improved. I remember asking a preschool teacher if I could leave him in time-out all day, because I was so tired. When I let him out of time-out, he got right back into trouble. It was exhausting.

He had a problem with entitlement. No matter what we did for him, in his mind, it was not enough. One year we took six of the kids on a vacation to Yellowstone National Park. He was one of only two children who went horseback riding, and whitewater rafting with some of the adults. We had a week of non-stop fun. On our way home, he was angry that we wouldn't buy him some trinket out of a novelty shop. His response to us was, "You never give me anything." I know that is coming from the mouth of a child, and children can be very selfish—and let's face it, they just don't get it. I would accept that, except that was his attitude every hour of every day. I had a hard time understanding where his entitlement came from. His cup of juice was never full enough, he never got enough food to eat, and he deserved more privileges than the other children, and so on. He was always complaining about what he didn't get.

He would lie about finished projects, or homework at school. He refused to work—even though he is brilliant. He chose never to put any effort into anything he did. Whether it was schoolwork, piano lessons, work around the house, it didn't matter. We couldn't even get him to take care of his folded laundry. Instead, he would throw it in the closet, under the bed, anywhere. Not a big deal in a small child, but it *never* stopped.

We did try counseling, but it didn't seem to do any good.

As he got a little older, he seemed to move from one bad behavior to another. We would catch him stealing. He would come home from school, and he would have a toy or game that didn't belong to him. Once, he actually had a $150.00 electronic device. I asked where he got it, and he said his friend gave it to him.

I asked, "Your friend just gave you his Christmas gift?"

He said, "Yes, but I gave him a jolly rancher candy in exchange." I think he thought I had *stupid* written on my forehead.

I went to school the next day, and asked the teacher. She said it had been reported stolen out of the other boy's backpack. This happened several times. He would come home with action figures, and he always told us his friends had given him the toys—when in reality, he had helped himself to their backpack when they weren't looking. It got to the point that when I went to bed at night, my purse was taken upstairs with me. We couldn't trust him to not steal from us.

He had a great knack for swindling people out of things he wanted. He sees a weak point in a person, and goes in for the kill. In his mind, that justifies his behavior. He can say that they gave it to him that way, when really he just swindled them out of it.

An example of this is he knows his sister Sarah has an eating disorder. He told her he would give her ONE potato chip for her brand new iPod that her biological sister had gotten her for her birthday. She agreed. She handed over her iPod, and she ate the potato chip. He was so angry when we made him give the iPod back. He really thought he had a *right* to have it.

One of the most frustrating behaviors that Mike exhibited was he never took responsibility for his actions. This bothered us, and was a little scary to deal with. He could get caught cheating—I mean actually *caught in the act*—and he would deny it, and rationalize it, even though he knew he was caught. He would look me right in the eye, and deny it over and over again.

When talking with some of his teachers, they would eventually laugh, because it was such an obvious thing, yet he would deny it to the bitter end.

He is the only child out of ten that has had detention at school, not once—but several times. We have received numerous phone calls from teachers because of behavioral problems during class.

My husband would explain time and time again how it was time for him to be a man. He needed to take responsibility for his actions. We told him everyone makes mistakes, we acknowledge our mistakes, and then learn from them so they don't happen again. We would give him several chances to come clean. It never happened. It didn't matter what he did wrong; he would never admit it.

He snuck out of the house many nights. We finally put a deadbolt lock on the garage so he couldn't get out anymore. One day, Tom had spent the whole day with him one-on-one. They went to Cabella's, and Tom bought him a bow and arrows, glove, and target. He came home, and Tom gave him one rule. He said, "This is a weapon, you can only shoot it at the target. Don't point it anywhere else."

Later that evening, Tom and I went out for our date night. The first thing Mike did, was start trying to hit birds out of the sky. His arrow ended up on another street, on a neighbor's roof.

When the babysitter told him to come in for dinner, he argued with her, and would not obey. For his defiance, she put him on kitchen-cleaning duty all by himself. He not only had to wash the dishes, he had to sweep the floor, and wipe the counters as well.

At the time, she was not aware that he had shot an arrow down the street. He didn't want her to know, because then she would tell us, and he would get into trouble. So, instead of asking her to go with him to the neighbor's house, he snuck away and went by himself.

He rang their doorbell, introduced himself politely, and told them he had shot his arrow on their roof, and could he please get it down. The neighbor went outside with him, and looked where the arrow had landed on his roof. He realized the arrow was on the tallest section of his roof, and he didn't have a ladder to get up to get it. He told Mike to come back the next day, bring his dad and a ladder with him, and he would be happy to let him up on the roof to get the arrow down.

This was a problem. Mike knew we would take away his bow and arrow if we knew he hadn't obeyed the rule to only shoot it at the intended target. Instead of coming clean, he decided to sneak out of the house around 11:30 P.M. He climbed from the neighbor's fence to his roof, and went and grabbed his arrow. When he climbed down, he also decided to toilet papered their house. After that, he hung out at a fast food restaurant until 2:00 A.M. in the morning.

The next day after church, we were resting in the living room when the doorbell rang. It was a police officer, and she was looking for the boy named Mike that owned the bow and arrow. We informed her that he lived here, and she asked if she could come in and speak to my husband and me for a few minutes.

We sat down with her in our front room while she relayed the story to us about the arrow ending up on the roof of the neighbor's, and about Mike showing up and asking if he could get it down. She told us what the neighbors told him, and that after the conversation with Mike, he went home.

Then she said the neighbors' heard a noise in the middle of the night, and they thought someone was breaking into their house. They were very frightened, and for their protection, they got their guns out. After a few minutes, they realized it was coming from their roof—not from the inside of their house.

When they woke up the next morning, they informed the police that the arrow was gone, and they knew who it was that had been on their roof. They wanted an apology, and they wanted to make sure we knew what had happened because Mike had put himself in a dangerous situation. They could have shot him.

We asked Mike to join us in the front room. When he walked in and saw the police officer, he looked a little pale. The officer talked to him and he knew he was busted. She explained that he had made a really bad choice, and he could have gotten himself, or someone else, hurt.

Tom was so hurt and so angry. He had to take Mike to the neighbors' to apologize. He also took away the bow and arrow. It was a hard day for my husband. He was at a loss. He wanted so desperately to get through to Mike, and he realized we weren't getting anywhere fast.

Even after this incident, Mike went around and told all the kids in the family that the babysitter had taken him to the neighbors. When they asked the neighbor if he could get his arrow down, they slammed the door in his face. He told them that that is why he had to get it in the middle of the night. We explained to the children that it was a lie, and we even had the sitter tell them that she never went to the neighbors' house, they never slammed the door in her face, and she didn't know the arrow was on the neighbor's roof. It was another incident where he refused to take responsibility for his actions, and just man up.

We couldn't find his currency. Nothing worked. Nothing changed his behavior: we could take away sports, take away privileges, spend more one-on-one time with him, offer grace, positive behavioral charts, talking, praying, natural consequences, everything we could think of—the behavior never stopped.

We became exhausted. We had never seen a child like this. Usually, you can train a child, and they respond and learn. With Mike, he never responded or learned. The difficulty of it was we never got a break from it. It was something different every day to deal with. We realized that we had eight children in the home, and Mike was taking 99% of our energy. The stress became huge. It was affecting our marriage, and the other children in the home. The other kids were doing exceptionally well, but our time and energy was mostly going to Mike. It was hard.

Mike is a valuable child that God created and loves very much. He is precious and worth more than he will ever know. He is also a sweet boy. He loves his sisters, and his family. He is funny and very likeable. He has unbelievable potential. He is so smart; he is athletically talented, musically talented, and cute as a button.

He has heart and integrity issues. We don't have the ability to change a person's heart. God does that, and Mike has had a hard time yielding to God's healing touch. Deep down, he wants to make good choices, and to this day we can't figure out why it is so hard for him. We love Mike. We had to make some drastic and difficult changes before we lost this child who was now 14 years old.

We had contact with Mike's uncle who lived in California, as well as his grandma. Mike also had another uncle that we had met, but didn't see. Mike's uncle knew of the problems we were having with Mike. He informed us that his brother Joe had wanted Mike from day one, and that he and his wife were turned down as a placement because she worked days, he worked nights and Mike would have to be put into daycare. They also didn't want to separate him from Joy, and CPS felt that he had been with us for so long he should stay here. They never told us Mike's uncle was another option for placement nine and a half years earlier.

We contacted his Uncle Joe and Aunt Chris who were now living in Kentucky. Joe was only 53, but had retired. They had bought a mini-farm, and Mike's grandma was planning to move there in the near future. They lived next to a large river where fishing was plentiful. We began developing a relationship with him.

He informed us that when Mike was taken away from his mother, the family wasn't contacted. They would ask Mike's mom where Mike was when he didn't show up at family get-togethers. His mom always had an excuse, like he was at a friend's house, or visiting his other grandparents. They believed her, until about a year went by and they still hadn't seen Mike. They approached her, and wanted the truth. She finally admitted that he had been taken away by the state.

They immediately contacted the state. They went to every court hearing. They made it known that they wanted Mike placed with them (we knew nothing of this). The state refused. They hired an attorney, and the attorney told them it would cost them about $40,000 to fight the case, and they would never win. They were furious.

On top of that, their sister died a month after her rights were terminated. Mike was the only part of their sister they had left. They were being told there was nothing they could do. They were so hurt.

We wish we would have known all this back at decision time. We would have insisted that Mike go live with them on day one, only because it would have been the right thing to do. It is all hindsight, and easy to say now. We do believe there is a reason Mike was placed with us, and hopefully, the nine and a half years he lived with us will someday make a difference in his life. We believe you plant the seed in people's lives, and God makes it grow. We know it was not an accident to God that he lived here.

We spent a lot of time discussing Mike's situation with his family. All of us that loved him (grandma, two uncles, an aunt and us) decided that it would be in Mike's best interest to go live with Uncle Joe in Kentucky. His uncle was retired, and would have more one-on-one time to invest in his life. Mike would be attending a smaller school, he would be with his mom's family, which is important to kids. These people are good and decent, hardworking people.

We agreed that when Mike left, we would call him once a week to see how he was doing. We would remain his parents; we would be getting help for him that he so desperately needed. He would come home for visits often, and we would also fly there to visit him. We did not take this decision lightly. We had to consider the other children in the home, and how this would affect them—especially Joy. We spent a lot of time talking, praying, and seeking counsel from a trusted few.

We had a lot of guilt. Were we agreeing to this just to *get him off our hands* because he was so difficult? Were we doing the right thing? What was our motivation? How would our friends and family respond? We did some real soul-searching, and finally concluded that moving him would be in everyone's best interest—especially Mike's.

His family was extremely excited, because they had wanted him from day one. They saw this as getting their family back together, and they couldn't wait. We made the decision in January that Mike would be moved when school was out in May. His uncle immediately began adding a bedroom onto his little cottage.

It was time to approach the subject with Mike. We prayed. We didn't want him to feel like we were giving him away. We had to choose our words very carefully. We also didn't want the other kids in the home to think that if they acted out, we would *give them away* as well. We didn't feel that we were *giving him away*. We were instead giving him another opportunity to have more adults pour good things into his life, and hopefully, he would respond positively. Even though we thought it was the right thing to do, it was still a difficult time.

One evening, my husband sat down to talk with Mike. He explained that we loved him very much. He told him the story of his mom's family, and that they had always wanted him. He said that we had all been talking, and his family wanted a chance to get to know him. His grandmother was planning to pay for his college, and she wanted an opportunity to spend some time with him before his college years.

We told him we could be selfish and keep him all to ourselves, or we could bless them. We explained that we were not giving him away. We would still be in control, and we would be in touch all the time to see how he was doing. We still wanted to be a big part of his life. We also explained that his uncle was retired, and had more time to invest in his life. We talked for a long time, and then asked him how he felt. He was crying, but he replied that he also thought it would be a good idea.

His uncle and grandma quickly made a trip out to see him. His uncle brought pictures of the farm, and we all went to dinner a couple of times with just Mike—so we could talk, and he could ask any questions he had. His family was very excited. His grandma must have said *thank you* to me a million times. She explained how the last nine years had been so sad for their family. They never wanted Mike to be placed in foster care, and they were so excited to get the chance to care for him themselves.

We also had to explain things to the other kids. We didn't initially say that he was moving to Kentucky. We told them that he was going to be visiting his uncle for the summer, and getting to meet some of his cousins. We wanted to get them used to the idea of him being gone. When summer was winding down, we explained that he was doing well, and so he was going to stay a little longer, and we would visit him on a school break. Everyone was fine with that.

It has been a little weird; we thought the transition of him leaving would be more difficult than it has been. The other kids in the home haven't asked for him or even stated that they miss him. When he is on the phone, the children who are available, talk with him and they seem to enjoy that very much. I once asked them if they notice any difference since he left. Every child that was asked said, "Yes, it is peaceful now," or "Yes, there is no more yelling," or "We are all laughing again." And indeed, the laughter is back in our home.

We sat down separately with Ted and Matt, and tried to explain the situation to them. They are older, and realized the struggles that we had and the effect it had on all of us, especially Tom and me. Matt supported our decision. He said, "If Ted had a son, and Ted died—I would do anything to have that kid in my care. I would never want it in foster care, or adopted out to another family. His family deserves to know him."

Ted on the other hand, didn't agree, but didn't make it difficult for us. He just said, "They are not his family, we are, and he should be with us." He still doesn't understand, but we have a peace about the decision that was made, knowing that it is in everyone's best interest. We did what we felt was best.

Before Mike left, I explained to him that this was a new beginning for him. He would have a clean slate. I explained that his uncle would trust him until he was untrustworthy. I encouraged him to go, and be a blessing to them. I wanted his high school years to be some of the finest years of his life. I encouraged him to not blow this opportunity to be with his birth family. I reminded him of who he is. He is not a liar or a thief. We went over all the gifts and abilities God had blessed him with. I reminded him how fortunate he was to have had dad invest nine years of his life teaching him how to be a man, and that Mike knows right from wrong. It was time for him to step up, and be a man. We talked and talked some more.

It was interesting how his attitude changed once he knew he was leaving. He would say things like, "When I get to Kentucky, my family is going to buy me an iPad; I am going to get a $500.00 phone, and anything else I want."

I said, "Do you think you're going to Candy Land? You aren't going to Kentucky so your family can buy you everything you think you need to have. You are going to Kentucky to get to know your family, be a blessing to your family, be blessed by getting to know them, and have another man invest in your life." He didn't believe me.

He was shocked when he got to Kentucky and he was not greeted with a $500.00 phone or an iPad.

Right before he left, he also said to me, "I hope my new family encourages me. I could use a little encouragement." I about died.

I made him look me in the eye, and I said, "Like, you don't need to steal. That's not who you are. You are better than that. Everything that you need, you have. You don't need to cheat in class. You are smarter than any kid I know. Just do your best that is all we ask. You don't need to lie. You are not a liar. Tell the truth, and take the consequences, good or bad, like a man." I went on for about ten minutes. Then I said, "The problem here, Mike, is that you refused to accept our encouragement, and therefore we had no choice but to administer discipline. Believe me, we have spent over nine years encouraging you to be all we knew you could be."

Some of the things that he was saying were hurtful, but we understood where it was coming from. We knew this was also difficult for him, and he didn't know how to express that.

One day in May, his uncle showed up with a moving truck. He was picking up Mike and his things, and then the two of them were heading to Las Vegas to pick up his grandmother's things to take with them to Kentucky. She would be following shortly after.

When it was time to say goodbye, he hugged Joy, but ignored Sarah. Matt and Ted were here, and so they were able to say goodbye, as well as Tom and I. He didn't seem upset about leaving, we all just reminded each other that we would see each other soon, and off he went.

The next day we realized that an iPad was missing. Cathy said when she walked into Mike's room the day before, she saw him throw an iPad under his dresser when she entered his room. She knew he was trying to hide it, but she didn't tell us. I realized that he had taken it with him, even though he knew he couldn't have it. It belonged to his older brother.

Talk about hurt. I sat and cried. I couldn't believe that this child stole from us on his way out of the house. I felt so disrespected. I was at a loss. When he called a few days later I said, "So, you took the iPad that was your brother's, huh?"

"Well, I guess," he replied.

"You did, or you didn't. Which is it?"

"I guess I did," he finally said.

I asked to speak to his uncle. I told his uncle he took the iPad, and it didn't belong to him. His uncle said, "Well, I wondered where he got it, because the four of us had discussed that he wasn't to have any electronic devices until we all saw how he did when he got there." He informed me that Mike had set up a Facebook account with a fake name, was emailing and taking and sending lots of pictures.

I told the uncle that I was so frustrated, that I didn't care what he did with the iPad. I said, "I don't care what you do, you decide. Let him keep it, send it back, whatever you feel is best. I just don't care." Talk about defeated.

The next time I spoke with his uncle, he informed me that he had a talk with Mike, and that the iPad had been taken away, and would be returned to us shortly.

Did things go the way we hoped? Not really. Remember, I said Mike has a heart-issue, and only Mike can fix the heart-issue. I thought there would at least be a honeymoon period with his uncle. There was not.

Within three months of being there, his uncle couldn't let Mike in the house if he wasn't in the house himself. Mike was proving himself untrust-worthy.

They made him quit the football team because of his behavior. Our hearts broke. His uncle continues to encourage and discipline him. We talk weekly, so we can discuss what is going on, and brainstorm together what needs to be done. We also talk to Mike weekly to try to encourage him.

After Mike had been there for six months, I received a call from his uncle. He informed us that he was *done*. He said it was to the point that he and his wife could hardly even look at him, and they wanted him gone as soon as possible.

Realistically, we had seen this day coming, but we were still taken aback when it actually occurred. We thought they would be able to handle him for at least a year, and when Mike left, we were hopeful that his family would be able to get through to him—and help him make some positive changes. It was just too much for them.

The day after the phone call, we purchased a one-way ticket for him to come home.

I will be honest, and say that for the first week after receiving the phone call, we were angry, and somewhat sick to our stomachs. I personally spent a lot of time crying, wondering how we were going to do it another three and a half years. I would lie awake for hours, asking God for insight and wisdom. I was anxious.

We talked to the kids, and most of them were excited for his return. Some were concerned the atmosphere in the house would change back to one of constant conflict. We assured them that we would not let that happen.

Once it began to sink in that he was really coming home, we had to change our thinking. We reminded ourselves that any time you are in ministry, and trying to do something positive—there will be opposition. We knew going into this—these kids were damaged, and it would be very difficult. Some kids never respond positively to the efforts being given on their behalf. That didn't change the fact that we had to continue to be faithful with the child God has graciously entrusted to us.

Tom and I have spent a lot of time talking about how we will ensure upon his return that it doesn't negatively affect the other children in the home—or our marriage. We have come up with some new guidelines for dealing with his negative behaviors, and how we are going to make sure we are both on the same page, working as a team.

Mike called us from Kentucky, and when I asked him how he felt about coming home, he said he was disappointed that he didn't do what he had set out to do. I told him not to be disappointed. I asked him if he had learned anything in the six months he had been gone. He responded that he had. I said, "So have we. Let's just start fresh." I reminded him that we loved him, God loved him, and that God had great plans for his life. I told him we were excited for his return, and couldn't wait to all be together as a family again. I assured him that when he got home—he was going to do very well. I believed in him. It would be good for him to be home where we can physically pray with him and encourage him daily to make good choices.

I am comforted with the fact that Jesus was able to walk on water. He raised the dead, and healed the sick. He promises that when we kneel before him, he will lift us up. He is able to give me the strength I will need, moment-by-moment, day in, and day out. Do I just say I believe in Him and His power, or will I choose to live my faith out and really trust God?

I made a decision that I will not be defeated. I will get up every day, and be faithful with what I have been called to do. I will love that child, nurture, protect, lovingly discipline, train, advocate, and guide him.

I don't know how this is going to turn out. Mike won't be home for another few weeks. I know that sometimes when things don't go as we plan, we can feel like we have failed. But then we have to change how we define success. If for nothing else, Mike knows right from wrong. He has a relationship with God, which can change the way he chooses to live.

Yes, it has been difficult from day one. I am encouraged by the fact that *never once* did we walk through this alone. God has been faithful every step of the way. He has given us wisdom, strength, and his perfect peace when we have needed it, and he will continue to guide, strengthen, and give us his wisdom when we ask.

Sometimes, things don't turn out how we think they will, or how we *wish* they would. But, nothing is a surprise to God. He knew that this would be difficult, and he has taught us so much through this experience.

The final chapter on Mike has not yet been written, and I am hoping and praying it is a chapter filled with only good things.

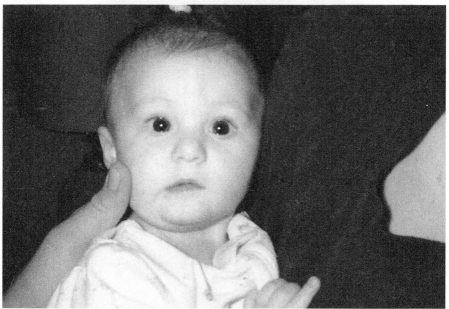

Mike at age five
Joy at age seven months

Mike and Joy ages thirteen and nine

Things you should know

You will never fix anyone: Most of the people getting into foster care feel that they have something to offer, and they probably do. These kids come wounded, some severely, some not so severely. But, they are all wounded. The reality of it is some of them will come wounded, you will house them wounded, and they will leave your care wounded. Hard to swallow, I know. It really hit us hard when we realized that we weren't fixing some behaviors that we personally thought were fixable. There have been times we felt like we are doing no good, and we just want to give up. We have to remind ourselves that the truth is—it is not our job to fix anyone. That is God's. It is our job to get up every day and care for these children. To be faithful parents who take the time to discipline, love and nurture these children. We are not responsible for the outcome, or how they respond. We are only called to be faithful with what we have been entrusted.

Develop tough skin: You will have some friends and family that will encourage you and support your decision to bring these kids into your home. Other people will think you are crazy and they don't mind sharing that with you. I had a pastor once, not at our church, tell me that he thought I was addicted to adopting kids. I asked him if he was crazy.

I said, "Who would be addicted to the sleepless nights because of nightmares, the youth that won't stop spitting in your face, as well as wallpaper being torn off your walls. A child that is 11, but can't put a period at the end of a sentence. An adolescent that masturbates while watching TV because it sooths them, or pulls out their eye brows. A teen that you have never held to your breast but you are expected to love like your own while they are stealing from you. I could go on and on."

By the time I was finished, the pastor assured me that what I was doing was most certainly because of my love for my Savior and because I was called to do it.

I got in the car and kind of chuckled to myself. He didn't know whom he was messing with!

Another time I was visiting a very good friend—who has been very supportive of our decision to bring the kids in, and she loves the kids—who told me I was too hard on them. I am hard on them. I don't tell people why we do certain things (no blanket while watching TV because of masturbation problems, etc.) because it isn't their business.

She continued to give me her opinion, and I politely said… "You live in your $750,000 house with your custom-made furniture. You can talk to me when you live one day in my shoes. You can't get it, because you don't do it."

Another time, I was at church and someone came up to me and said, "Why would they give you another kid?"

My brother also consistently tells us how crazy we are. I appreciate people's opinions, but I also know they can't understand if they aren't living it. They see from the outside. They see your kids on Sunday morning, dressed in their finest, with their hair done beautifully, and they can't even imagine the issues you have had to deal with that week. They don't need to know. I just tell them to please pray for us.

If it is possible scrapbook with your kids: Our kids all have scrapbooks. I am reminded of a funny story. Paul came to live with us on December 9. He was 13 years old, and he does have autism. The first of January, I was done with their Christmas page. That was all he had in his scrapbook. He was looking at his page, and he was laughing and saying, "Oh, these are such great memories." I thought how sweet, your memories aren't even two-weeks-old and they are precious to you. All of our kids get a page for their birthday, Christmas, school year, vacation, religious ceremonies, piano recitals, camps, adoptions, broken bones, etc. and of course a birth family page. They will cherish these books when they get older. If you can, get pictures of them before they came to live with you. Paul and Sarah have no pictures of themselves until they were nine and 13. They would love to know what they looked like as babies. If they were in another foster family before they entered your house, ask that family if they have any pictures of them so you can add that to their books.

You may have difficulty bonding: Bonding is a weird thing. I have found that bonding is also a subject many adoptive parents feel guilt about, and don't want to talk about. As I share my experience with them, I have heard a lot of "I am so thankful you said that to me. That is exactly how I feel, but feel ashamed to voice it." So, let's talk about it openly and honestly.

Firstly, it is critical to bonding that a child has bonded with a significant person in their life before coming to you. Bonds can be transferable. If a child has bonded with a person, such as a parent or caregiver, they can usually transfer that bond to another. If you are having trouble bonding with a child it could be because the child is unable to bond with you. You can't get mad at a deaf person for not hearing. They are incapable of hearing. You can't make them hear. Some of these kids are incapable of bonding—no matter what you do, or how hard you work to bond with them.

Second, women bond with a child by carrying them in their womb. We hold them close to our breast, rock them, sing to them, stay up with them all night while they are sick, play games with them, etc..... Do we do that with a thirteen, eleven, five or nine-year-old that has been dropped off at our house? Of course not. Then on top of that, they come with behaviors that can drive you crazy.

It is not an easy thing to bond with older children, and feel like you would feel had you gotten them as an infant. I care very much for all my children. Do I love them all the same? Here goes, "No, I do not." Some of them I feel more like a life-coach then like a mom. Whether they can't bond with me or me with them, is insignificant. The fact is there is a lack of bonding. It is brutal to deal with the guilt.

I have struggled severely with one of my kids. I have cried many tears and have begged God to give me a love for them—a love that a mother has for a child. It has never come. It is a struggle. I finally stopped feeling guilty, and accepted it for what it is. Is it what I wanted? Is it a sad fact that this child has been short changed in life? It is called adoption. It is a part of adoption that we don't like to talk about.

I know people who have adopted siblings, and struggle bonding with one of them and live in terrible guilt over it. I think it's time we talk about it, we get rid of the guilt, we pray for one another, we encourage one another to do the best that we can do with what we have been given.

Believe it or not, they may not be thankful: I guess I thought the kids would be thankful for the sacrifice we have made. Some of the kids are, and some are not. I think about the piano lessons, braces, vacations, clothes, nice house, no abuse, sports participation, and all the other stuff we give them. I thought they would be thankful to be in a safe environment with parents that are attentive: parents that help them with their homework, and interact with them in a positive way. It was hard at first to realize that they would prefer to be with their biological family, even as unhealthy as it was. It was their normal—and their normal is comfortable and secure to them. We get it, but it isn't always easy. Also, we didn't take them in for a *thank you.* We realize they owe us nothing. Again, we chose to take them in. They didn't choose us.

If you are married, tag team: people usually marry opposites. There is a reason for that. If we were alike, then one of us would be unnecessary. My husband's strengths tend to be my needs, and vice versa. He is really good at showing the kids grace and not getting freaked out by some of their behaviors. I on the other hand, always freak out first and then figure out what to do. When there is an issue that has to be dealt with quickly, he is the better one to handle that. When there is an issue where tough love needs to be administered, then I handle that. When one of us needs a break, the other one can step up, so we don't get burned out. My husband and I make it a point to have date night every Saturday night. We also get away for weekends about four times a year. We take a trip alone once a year that lasts a week. It is so important that we have a healthy relationship. When the kids move out, it is just the two of us.

Even the ugly memories are special to them: This title cracks me up, because it is true for some of the older kids. We were watching the show, "Infested." It is a show about people whose houses are invested with different critters. One house was infested with roaches. Sarah tells me that the house they lived in with their parents was infested with roaches, like the house we were seeing on TV. I said, "Well you probably had roaches, but not like these houses that are totally infested." She assured me, and had Paul back it up, that *yes* their house was infested with roaches.

She got the biggest smile on her face, and giggled like a little girl telling the most precious memory of how there were roaches running all over the place, and they would play a game every day to see who could count the most roaches. She would get more than 1,000 in a day. She didn't mind the roaches, only when they fell off the ceiling into her food. My first thought was, how she can ever complain in my house—she has yet to have a roach fall into her food.

I have a friend who has adopted two children. Her kids lived under a bridge, and never even went to school. They remember their dad bringing them relish packets like it was a trip to Disneyland. My friend said, maybe I should just wrap up relish packets for them at Christmas. That seems to get them more excited than anything else.

You will need a support system: It is very important that you have a good support system. You will have friends and/or family tell you how crazy you are for taking in children and giving up your freedom (if that is the case). You will have people want to give advice when they don't understand what it is like raising children who are not yours, and who come with issues they have never dealt with. It is like anything else in life. You don't really understand until you experience it first-hand.

We went to classes and parties at our agency, and we met other foster and adoptive parents who really can get it. It is important to have someone to talk to who won't judge how you feel, and can encourage you in what you are going through. You will also have to be reminded of the truth. These kids are precious, and they deserve a family, and our time and sacrifice. They are not throwaway children.

We have a few families who we get together with regularly, and those are the friends who we can talk to about the stuff that no one else would get—unless they were living it themselves. My advice would be to have other adoptive/foster parents as part of your support system. I really think that is a critical aspect to being successful.

Try to embrace their culture: This was a difficult one for me. I didn't really realize the importance of embracing their culture. I will not be politically correct in saying this, but I use to joke that I would take my Mexican- American children to Taco Bell once a week and buy them a taco. I felt that they had a good, safe, loving home, and it was enough. This area was definitely a need for me.

Once I began to realize the importance of culture, my thinking changed. Embracing a child of another race's culture doesn't have to be difficult. We have piñatas for some of their birthdays now. I make red beef enchiladas now, instead of just the chicken.

It wasn't long after Sarah came to live with us that I was dropping her off at school. She asked me what I was going to be doing when I got home.

I said, "Making enchiladas for dinner." Sarah loves food, and she talks with her hands.

She replied, "Enchiladas, oh, I love enchiladas."

I said, "Good." She then asked me—with both hands going at once—if I was making enchiladas so that we could communicate.

I started to laugh and I said, "No, I made enchiladas before you came to live with us. We all love enchiladas. But we will be communicating. I will be telling you to stop licking your plate." I came home, and made the enchiladas.

When it was time for dinner, Sarah was standing by the stove as I removed dinner from the oven. She took one look at the food and she said, "What is that?" She had a disgusted look on her face.

I replied, "Enchiladas, remember you love enchiladas."

She looked closely at dinner, and reported to me that what I made was surely *not* enchiladas, because it looked nothing like the enchiladas her Nana use to make. I realized that she was used to the red enchiladas, and so it was then that we added those to the menu. And by the way, she loved the chicken ones as well.

My point is that whenever it is possible, incorporate some of the food, customs, and holidays into your family so that they know that their culture is important to you.

Don't raise them to be victims: We will all experience pain in our lifetimes. We live in a world where bad things happen, and life can be, and is, very hard. I want my kids to know that it is in the times when we face the greatest pain, that we see more clearly the love of God. Being older, I can look back and see that out of the difficulty of pain I have experienced, has come strength, and compassion to help others. These kids have been through a lot. It is our job to try to help them deal and work through the pain so that they can be stronger people, able to help others with what they have learned, forgive, and move into healthy adulthood.

I am reminded of a true story that I once heard at a concert. There was a pastor who was a daredevil. He liked to jump out of planes, rock climb, etc.... He had a friend that was a heart surgeon. He asked his surgeon friend on many occasions if he could witness a heart surgery. Finally, the friend told him he could, but he wasn't allowed to speak one word during the surgery, and he had to stand in the back of the room. The pastor agreed, and the day of the open-heart surgery finally arrived. The surgeon began surgery by opening a women's chest. He took the heart out, mended it, and put it back in. Apparently, to get a heart beating again after you have repaired the damage, you massage it. So, the surgeon massaged the heart, but it didn't start beating. He massaged it again, which also didn't work. An amazing thing then happened. The surgeon moved to the woman's head, got down on his knees, and whispered into her ear, "Mrs. Johnson, I have repaired your heart, and now I need you to make it beat. Mrs. Johnson, please make your heart beat." They waited a few seconds, and the heart started beating on its own. It truly was a miraculous moment for the pastor to witness.

He likens that to our hearts being broken, hurt, untrusting, and unwilling to love. When we ask, God repairs our hearts, and then whispers into our ear ever so quietly, "I have repaired your heart, and now I need you to make it beat." These kids have experienced hurt, mistrust, and a lack of love. They need to know that they are not victims. That God has repaired their heart and they need not be afraid to let it beat again. Learn to love, trust, and to fully heal. There is hope in every situation, and we don't want their pain to be wasted.

Teach them there is a God of impossibilities, and that he is able to make miracles happen. He will not let us fall; there is nothing too hard or impossible for God.

Celebrate special days: When Cindy and Cathy had been our daughters for ten years, I decided that I should celebrate that day. The girls were aware that they had been in our family for ten years as we had been talking about it. They both attended a very small Christian school that I volunteered at daily. It was not weird for them to see me at school every day. So, on the ten-year-anniversary of them coming into our family, I stopped at the store and got them each a bouquet of flowers, cupcakes for the class, as well as a sweet card. I proceeded to Cathy's sixth grade class first. When she saw me, she just giggled. The kids all thought it was her birthday.

I said, "No, it's not her birthday, but Cathy tell them what today is."

She told them that she had been adopted ten years earlier and they all thought that was really cool. I handed out cupcakes, thought that went well, and I moved on to Cindy's seventh grade room.

When I walked into Cindy's room, they were working quietly at their desks. Her teacher said, "Oh, do we have a birthday today?"

Cindy replied that it wasn't her birthday.

The teacher asked, "Then what is the special occasion?"

Cindy said, "I don't know."

I was standing in front of Cindy's desk and I said, "Cindy, you don't know what today is?"

She replied, "No, I have no idea."

I stood there for probably only a few seconds, and I watched the realization come upon her. She began rubbing her eyes and within a minute, she was crying as she told the class that it had been ten years since she had gotten a family. She lost it, and was crying, which made me cry—and we were both blubbering, while the class was clapping and I got to say…

"Cindy, I prayed for a daughter, and since the day you came into my home you have done nothing but bring me joy. From the moment I looked into your big, brown eyes, I loved you. I am so blessed, and so thankful that you are my daughter." It was a moment the two of us will never forget. Even the teacher said later that it was the sweetest thing he had ever seen. And that is coming from a man!

If adoption occurs, throw one massive party: With all our kids we have done something special for their adoption. We always buy them a new and special outfit. With Sarah and Paul, we invited Paul's seventh grade class to the actual adoption at the courthouse, and then we took them and Sarah's fourth grade class out for pizza. For David, we had our pastor over and David was baptized in the backyard pool. For Mike, Mara, Joy, Cindy, and Cathy we had a huge buffet at the house. We invited everyone. Our pastor came over, we sang songs, had a video made of them that we showed, and the kids were dedicated to the Lord in a religious ceremony. We took lots of pictures to put in their scrapbook. If you adopt a child, always be sure to ask the judge if you can take a picture up by his bench. They are always happy to comply with that request, and it makes a great remembrance picture.

You may need to take special precautions: Our family is six families combined into one. We try to run like a *normal* family. The truth is—we are not. There are boys living here that are not truly related to some of the girls. We would like to ignore that fact, and pretend they are all blood brothers and sisters, but we cannot do that.

A boy that is brought in at age 13 is aware of the cute girl who lives in the house and that she is not really his sister. So, we have some special rules. We are fortunate enough to have a house set up perfectly for our situation. There are two bedrooms and one bathroom in the basement. Upstairs, there are three bedrooms and two additional bathrooms. The girl's rooms are upstairs, and the boys are downstairs. We do not allow the boys to go upstairs unless given permission. If the bathroom downstairs is taken, and there is an emergency, the boys will ask to use the upstairs bathroom. They never go upstairs without permission.

We had a situation with one of the boys, and for further protection (whether needed or not) we had French doors put in downstairs, and had an alarm put on the doors and we would set that alarm once the kids were in bed. If the boys left the downstairs in the middle of the night, the alarm would sound, and wake us up. We didn't do this until the kids were adopted. Because we don't have all the history on the kids, and don't know all of their background and experiences we have to be careful. We don't want anything horrible to happen on our watch. I wish that wasn't the case, but it is. It is one of the realities of bringing in foster children.

We are also very careful about dress. The girls have to wear bras even with their pajamas until they are in their room for the night. We watch what shorts they have on, and how they sit while we are all watching TV before bed. The girls are only allowed to wear one-piece bathing suits. It is not a bad thing. It teaches modesty at an early age, and will hopefully follow them into adulthood.

As a foster child, we never let our children sleep over at other people's houses. These kids have heard things, and some are street smart. You don't want them going to a house and sharing information that is not appropriate with other children. It protects them and you.

Don't be afraid to have them work: Most of these kids have come from homes where there is little responsibility. We call ourselves *Team Norton,* and everyone is a part of the team from the first day they enter the house. The kids are given responsibilities from the start. They have to make their bed, and keep their room clean. If they make a mess, they clean it up. They take care of their own animals. The boys are responsible for the yard work, and taking out the garbage. The girls work more on the inside of the house. We have a rotation every night for dish duty. One child does dishes, one sweeps the kitchen, and the other one wipes the counters. It switches by age every night. When we clean the house, we turn the music up and goof around while cleaning. Even the little children are given a chore or two. It sometimes would be much easier if I did it myself, but I want them to feel good about a job well done, and I want them to feel part of a team as they learn to work together to accomplish a task.

Be predictable, structured and organized: I need to have order in the home—otherwise, there is chaos. I am the one that makes sure the family runs smoothly. I probably go overboard on this one, but it works. Let me give you some examples: Breakfast is at 7:00 a.m. on school days, and 8:00 a.m. on weekends. Lunch is at noon, and dinner is at 5:00 p.m. It never changes. Bed-time is at 8:00 p.m. for the little ones, 9:00 p.m. and 10:00 p.m. for the older children. On weekends, they don't sleep past 7:30 a.m. They get to stay up a little later on the nights that are not school nights.

I get up and shower before the kids are out of bed, so that I am refreshed and ready to go. Once I send them to school, I usually get dinner together. I will make the lasagna, barbeque beef, casseroles, etc.… and put it in the refrigerator until time to stick it in the oven. That way, when the kids get home from school they have my attention. I can help with the baths (that calms them down, and gets them ready for dinner and homework), piano, and homework as well as listen to how their day at school went.

When they get home from school, there is also a system. The kids know to fill their water bottles, and get two items for their lunch the next day. They empty their backpacks, so I can go through them while they are practicing piano or resting for a bit.

My husband and I make it a point to both try to be here in the evenings—unless there is a sporting event the kids are in. If we are both here, it is much easier to tag-team helping with homework. We go from one child to the next until the work is complete. Sometimes, we ask an older child to help a younger one with their math if they are finished with their work. The TV is not turned on until all homework is complete.

Another thing that has been very helpful is having a clothes and shoe closet. The girls had a piano teacher that only shopped at the expensive stores, and she had three girls of her own. When she wanted to sell their clothes, she always called me first. I bought all of them. The clothes were like brand new. I got Christmas dresses, shoes that had only been worn one or two times, and perfectly good jeans, shirts and pajamas. I also had friends whose older kids gave us their hand-me-downs. These clothes were in great condition.

I put the clothes in containers with lids, and I label them. They will say *size 10 summer*, or *size 12 winter*. When we need clothes, we pull down the containers and go through them. When our older girls grow out of some of their clothes, the clothes are put in a container, and they get labeled for when the younger children are old enough to wear them. We also have a place in the upstairs closet for shoes. They are arranged by size. When the kids need a pair of dress or tennis shoes—before we buy them a new pair—they are sent to the closet to see if there is a pair in there that will fit them. It would be much more difficult if it wasn't organized. It runs really well.

Allow them to go through the grieving process: Grief is weird. There are steps to the grieving process, and not always done in the same order. We may think our kids have grieved all they are going to, but there may be some trigger that sets them off again. When Cathy met her biological dad, it triggered Cindy into grieving for the fact that she didn't get to meet her biological father. It's possible that when my children have kids of their own, they may struggle once again with all the *whys*. They need to know that how they feel is always okay, and then help them deal with those feelings in a healthy way. We don't want them to ever cause harm to themselves, or others, because of the severity of their pain.

Take care of yourself: Make sure you are taking care of yourself and your marriage. Let's face it—things can get tough. Make sure if you are married that your spouse comes first. Have a date night every week or two. Try to get away for an entire weekend every quarter.

Advocate for your child: You have to be your child's greatest cheerleader. You know their needs better than most, and so it is your job to fight for them. Our daughter Joy has a learning disability in math and reading. She was attending a small school where they had a teacher work one-on-one with her, and a few other children in the afternoon. They ended up alleviating that job, and Joy was left with no resources. We went to the principal who, after a lot of talking, just validated for us that fact that there were no resources for Joy to get the help she needed. So, it was a very difficult decision, but we moved Joy to the public school system where she could get the resources to help her with her disabilities. The other children did very well at the small private school. It was a blessing for us, because the teachers were always available. They knew us very well, and worked very closely with Tom and me to ensure that the children were reaching their full potential. They knew we disciplined our children, and they weren't afraid to talk to us about any problem, whether big or small.

We also knew Paul had autism, and that he also needed resources when starting high school. I contacted his school counselor who informed me there was nothing they could do for him, except possibly tutor him in the morning before school. I thought, "Are you crazy?" So I wrote a certified letter to the school asking them to assess Paul, knowing that once they received that letter they had 30 days to respond. He is now in special education classes, and they help him with his communication and social skills. Fight for your kids when you know there is a reason to fight.

Prepare them financially for living on their own: When our boys were growing up, they loved to make their own money. By the time they were 14, they were mowing several of the neighbor's lawns, and they would split the money. When they were 16 or 17, they had enough money to buy their first vehicle.

A lot of these kids aren't use to working, and would rather just take a handout. We support the idea that if you are capable of working, then you work. Paul has a disability, and I knew that it would probably be more difficult for him to find a job because he struggles socially. I sent him out anyway. I practiced with him what to do and what to say. He went to all the fast food restaurants in the area. My husband wasn't so sure this was a good idea. He didn't think anyone would hire him.

I told my husband, "Well he isn't living with me forever, so he has no choice but to get a job." It took about a month, but Paul finally got called in for an interview. He was hired, and he has worked there for two years now. When he gets his paycheck, we give him $40.00 and then we put the rest in a savings account that we have control over. He gets a little extra for vacations or extra activities that may come up. When he graduates from high school, and is ready to move out—he will have between ten and fifteen thousand dollars saved. That will be a good start.

Our second adopted son didn't appreciate the fact that we expected him to work—whether it was a job on the weekend, mowing lawns, babysitting, or whatever. He thought playing sports in school was work enough. It was kind of cute.

He said, "Don't I do enough?"

I replied, "Yes, you do enough recreation, and now you need to begin planning for your future." He loves to spend every dime he makes. We will not let him. We take his money, give him a little, and save the rest for him. He will be thankful when it comes time to move out, and he has some money.

One of the problems with him is he knows he has birth family who will take him in, let him lay on their sofa, and live off of them. We don't agree with that philosophy.

When the kids were little, we bought a bank that had three slots in it. One slot was for spending, one for saving, and one for giving. It taught them at a young age how to manage money. As it gets closer to them moving out, we will teach them budgeting and all the things they need to know to handle their money properly.

You will never be totally prepared for what lays ahead: When the children come into your home, expect them to come with little else then the clothes on their back. You will get a phone call, and you will either be told a small amount of information—that may or may not be correct—or you may be given a few more details regarding the child they are asking you to take. You will be asked to make that decision rather quickly. When we filled out paperwork, we were asked what age child we were willing to take in, and what behaviors we were willing to deal with. You need to know that the person calling you regarding the child cannot give you much information on the child, because they don't have that information to give. You will not know the extent of abuse, or the behaviors the child is exhibiting, until that child is in your home. You need to be aware of this. I had a friend who received a child—not knowing anything about the child—and when she got there, she was practicing witchcraft, and was a cutter. She didn't sign up for that, but what do you do? I was told several of our children had no behavioral issues. Really? Why did I believe that? They are in the system, mostly because of neglect and abuse. Do we think they could possibly have no issues? Be prepared to not know what you are going to deal with—and pray ahead of time, that God would give you the child or children that he has specifically assigned to your care.

The birth parents may see you as a threat: We realize that foster care is temporary, and that the goal is to reunite the child with their parent. Think about how you would feel if a stranger entered your home (the state) and took your children without your permission. How awful that would be. It is horrible for these parents. Most of them love their children, and are raising them the only way they know how. Into the picture you come. You probably drive a better car, wear nicer clothes, have a nicer house, and they see their child doing very well in your care. They think you are the one responsible for taking their child away from them. We sometimes think they will appreciate the care we are giving their child. It can be just the opposite. They can view you as a threat to their parenting, and their relationship with their child; therefore, it will be very difficult to form a relationship with them—which would be in the best interest of the child. You don't want the child to have divided loyalties. This happened with Mike, and is discussed in his chapter. You can, with the case-worker's permission, include them in parent-teacher conferences, give them pictures, copies of report cards, invite them to ball games, etc.… You have to make sure it is safe to do that beforehand. Even doing all that doesn't ensure that the parents will embrace what you are doing for their child. It can be very difficult to be seen as a threat by the biological parents.

Have family meetings: One of the things that have worked very well for us is *family meetings,* and we have them a couple of times a week. These were really nice when first bringing new children into the home, because it was an adjustment for everyone. We gather in a circle, and give everyone time to speak. We ask how they are doing. We want to know what things are going well, and what are not. What are the struggles everyone is experiencing? We make these meetings open and honest. We then take time to talk with the kids, and work out any issues they are having among themselves. We end with everyone praying together. It brings the family together.

Know your limit: This was hard for us. We knew we were called to care for these kids, but how many kids? We have such a heart for them, and want to take as many as we can. It is such a blessing to watch a child come into our home and get better in all areas of their life. When we took David, we also took his little brother and sister. We had them for six months, before handing them over to another adoptive family. We realized that is was too much for us. With his brother, I had two five-year-olds, and a four-year-old. My two kids did not like him. They continually harassed him. He had so many behavioral issues, and I didn't have the time to give him the care he needed, because I had too many kids. Twice, we left the little girl in the car, thinking someone else had brought her in. We were so thankful it was in the winter, or God only knows what would have happened. It was a difficult decision to let them go, but it was the right one. They are now the only two kids, in a family that tried to have kids of their own for 15 years. They get all the care they need, and they are doing great! They only live two miles away, and so David can visit them often. After that happened, we realized we could not take any more children into our home. We would have to help in other ways. Our quiver was full!

By all means laugh: Laugh and then laugh some more. You will be dealing with some very difficult issues. The day to day can get discouraging and tiring. Many nights, when Tom and I are laying our heads down after a long day, and as we talk about the day's events, we crack up. We laugh so we don't cry. We laugh about the funny, the stupid, the crazy, the cute, and sometimes we make jokes at each other for the way we handled a specific situation. You have to laugh at yourself and the kids. You don't want to go crazy, or focus too much on the challenges that you are facing. If someone heard what we are laughing about, they might think we are crazy. Some of the stuff just isn't funny. So, we make sure we laugh in the privacy of our room where nobody knows. It seriously keeps us sane at times.

Don't let your circumstances rob you of your joy: We were dealing with Sarah and one of her issues that is ongoing. I think to myself sometimes: *new day, same crap.* It is what it is, and you can't change some things, no matter how much you desire things to be different. On this occasion, I started laughing.

Sarah says to me, "Oh, and you laugh at that?"

I said, "Well, I can laugh, or what is my other option?"

She replied, "You can chuckle?"

I said, "No, I can laugh, or I can cry, and I chose to laugh."

Do not let the circumstances you are dealing with take away your joy. There is positive in everything. There are blessings heaping down upon all of us every single day. Thank God for the good, bad, ugly, hard, and everything in between. It will change how you view your circumstances, and your joy will remain intact.

Don't label or treat them like foster children: Don't introduce them as foster children. Don't say, "These are my two children, and these are my foster children." When people ask you if they are yours, your response should be,

"Yes." They are yours for a season, and we don't want the kids to feel less than part of the family. They don't want to be labeled.

You also need to make sure you dress them well. Don't give them worn-out clothes and shoes. Do their hair. When we all go out together, we sometimes get someone asking us if all the kids are ours. We never say, "Yes, we have two children, and eight adopted children." We have ten children.

Tom and I were once on a vacation together, and a lady asked me how many children I had. I told her ten. I then went to the bathroom, and when I returned she said, "Oh, you told me you had ten children, but your husband told me you had two children and adopted eight."

I replied, "Yes, two plus eight is ten. I have ten children."

Also, the kids have a right to privacy. Don't go telling everyone all their business. Be very selective about what you say, and to whom you say it.

Make sure you treat the foster children in your home the same as your biological children. I have known some foster families where there are different rules for bio/foster kids. Don't think the kids don't catch the injustice in that. If you can't treat them fairly, then they shouldn't be in your home.

Do not adopt them because of faith: We have watched some couples who are quite old make a decision to adopt, because they are afraid that the adoptive family won't have the same faith as they do. I get it. The two kids we let go to be adopted elsewhere was very difficult. I knew if they stayed with us, they would be safe and they would grow up in a Christian home which is very important to us. There is an age where you really shouldn't be adopting young children. There is a time when your quiver is full. When we were in a staffing picking out the family that would adopt two of our foster children, I had to remind myself that these kids did not belong to me. I was not the one that was going to save them. God draws all men unto himself. These children belong to God. Trust Him with their lives.

There are many ways to help children: There is a shortage of families in this country that are willing to take in foster kids. It can be frustrating, because I wish that more Christians especially would step up. But, it is not for everyone. There are so many ways to help these precious kids without bringing them into your home. If you know anyone with foster kids, volunteer to babysit for them occasionally. Pray for those of us who do it on a daily basis. Volunteer at the foster/adoption agency, or a shelter. Almost anyone can rock a crack baby. Get involved. You will be blessed!

Your child may be targeted simply because they are or were a foster child: Let me give an example. One evening, Tom and I got a call from the principal at the kids' school. He informed me that one of my children had been "molesting" another little girl on the playground. He told me which girl it was that was violated. He informed me that it had happened more than once. He was going to set up a meeting with the other parent, and with us for the following Monday. I hung up, and about died. I could hardly move to get to Tom to share what I had just heard. I couldn't believe what I was hearing. She was one of our children whom we had had for a very long time, and we would never suspect something like this out of her. I believe she was in the third grade, maybe the fourth grade at this time.

Later that evening, Tom and I met with her privately and we asked her questions in a roundabout way, seeing if we could get some information out of her, but she wasn't giving anything up. Later that evening, the mother of the child that was supposedly violated called me regarding some parent meeting. I was shocked that she said nothing of the "molestation."

So, I said, "Hey, shouldn't we be talking about something else. Like my daughter touching your daughter?" That started a conversation that shocked me. My child wasn't molesting her child. My child hit her child in the bottom, and said, "Hurry up," as they were running out to the playground. Her friend just wanted her to stop hitting her in the bottom. What a relief. All we had to do was explain to our daughter about boundaries, and that it isn't okay to touch someone's bottom to hurry them along.

I called the principal, who then apologized. He admitted that he jumped to conclusions, because *he knew my child was a former foster child*. He jumped to a conclusion before getting the facts. He then called us and used the word, "molested," which sent shock waves through our body. I explained to him that he had kids now, and how would he feel if he was the one on the receiving end of a phone call like that. We were so relieved.

Don't have expectations: I have found this one to be easier for the men. My husband will tell me that we have each other, and our two biological boys. Anything beyond that is just icing on the cake. I think because we women give so much of ourselves, our time, and emotions, that it is more difficult to not have expectations. Don't expect them to desire you over their birth family. Don't expect them to be thankful for all you have done. Do your work as unto the Lord, without wanting anything in return. Don't expect them to respond positively to your directions, love, care, discipline, time, money, or anything else. You will be disappointed at some point. Don't expect them to function at a certain level. They will function in life, but maybe not how you desire.

There is a tremendous emotional toil: Unfortunately, the system is broken. You may attend a permanency placement hearing, thinking a decision is to be made only to find out it has been extended another few months. It is very emotional watching things go on and on, having no control, or say in the matter, knowing that the poor child will continue to be in limbo. Your heart aches for the child.

I wrote a chapter regarding the system, but let me just say that working as part of the team is not always easy. In every job, you have good workers and not so good workers. It is the same for the job of the social worker. When you get a good social worker that is on top of the case, it is sweet. When you get one that is overworked, underpaid, and exhausted, it can be hard. They may not come and visit the child. They may not answer your emails or phone calls, and you may have a hard time getting services for the child. All of those things can be frustrating, and they take an emotional toll on you.

You will also hear things regarding the birth parents, or family, that will make your skin crawl. One of the most difficult aspects of foster care is staying focused. Before you begin, you think you can do it. After you hold that abused child in your arms, it becomes much more difficult to stay focused.

There is also the issue of visits. Statistics do show that visits with their family are beneficial for the child, even if it doesn't seem beneficial to us. This can be an emotional time for the child as well as yourself. It has been our experience that parents aren't always consistent in showing up for visits. I learned quickly not to tell the child ahead of time that they had a visit with their parent. That way, if the visit didn't happen we didn't have to deal with all the disappointment. It can be emotional for us, because we don't understand why these parents continually disappoint the child. It is also emotional, because if the child does have a visit, a lot of times they come home a mess afterwards. It can sometimes take three days to get the child back on track. They become an emotional mess, and it is hard to watch and deal with.

Give them experiences to remember: A lot of these kids haven't experienced some of the happy and simple things in life. I remember when we got Sarah, and she was going up to the cabin for the first time.

She saw the pine trees and she said, "Is this a real forest?"

I said, "Yes, have you never been to a forest?" She hadn't, and so at the age of ten she was beside herself with excitement. A lot of our kids had never seen snow, and so a simple trip up north was a big deal for them.

For Christmas, we don't buy gifts. We make memories. Let me explain. We make hot chocolate and cookies, and we load in the van and go to Sun City, which is a place where elderly people live. We go door-to-door Christmas caroling, and before we leave, we share our goodies with them. On that same night, we go looking at Christmas lights.

Then, on Christmas Eve we have a scavenger hunt. We divide into two teams: the older boys, and our friend's kids lead the two teams. They have video cameras and they are given a time limit. They will have a list of about 10 things to complete in their time frame. The list changes from year to year, and it is always a much-anticipated time. They may have to get someone to sing *Joy to the World* with them. They have had to read the story of the birth of Jesus to someone out of the Bible, complete an act of kindness for a stranger, get their picture with a nativity scene, buy shaving cream and get a picture with all of them having Santa beards and so on. When they finish, they come home and we watch their video and laugh like crazy while eating chocolate-covered pretzels.

Christmas morning, they open a custom-made shirt that gives clues to what their Christmas experience is going to be for that year. One year, they opened up shirts all together that said, "Team Norton Christmas family vacation." They had to guess where we were going for our Christmas vacation—and yes, it was Disneyland. None of them had ever been, and it was a hoot! We packed up on the 26th of December, and we were off for the vacation of every kid's dream.

This year, the boys opened up a shirt that said, "Look out below" and on the back were their name and a picture of someone parachuting out of a plane. You guessed it; their experience for the year was a tandem jump out of an airplane. You talk about a memory not easily forgotten.

The girls had a different shirt because their Christmas experience was going to be different than the boys. This year their shirt said, "Let's have a whale of a good time." On the back is a picture of a whale and their name. We were taking them to SeaWorld, a place they had never been. If the adventure is a hot air balloon ride the shirt says, "Up, up, and away" with a picture on the back of a huge balloon. If it is a train ride through the mountains, the shirt has a train on the back with a catchy phrase on the front. You get the idea. It is so much fun to plan each year and watch the kid's expressions as they realize what experience they are going to have.

The kids also don't exchange gifts every year. They each put $20.00 in a pot, and then they pick an experience to do all together. Last year, it was a place called *Jump Street* where they have indoor trampolines. After they finished, they all went out for Mexican food. Another year they went and played laser tag together before agreeing on a restaurant. All ten kids spend the day together, and you can bet it is better than getting a pair of socks you never really wanted to begin with.

We don't waste our money on electronics, games, or anything that will break or get old. We want them to look back and remember the experiences. It is neat having a shirt that goes with every event. The pictures are also put into their scrapbook. Always have a camera handy.

Nature versus Nurture: This is a highly debated subject. I cannot say I know the answer as to whether nature wins out over nurture, or vice versa. I can only tell you what we have experienced with our children. Our biological sons are a spitting image of Tom and me. One is exactly like Tom: he looks like Tom, acts like Tom, and is a miniature Tom. Our other son looks and acts like me. You can say, "Well, they act like you, because they lived with you." That is a good argument.

My parents raised us kids in Phoenix, Arizona while our relatives lived in upstate New York. When I was an adult, I took a trip back east to visit my grandmother. My mom's older sister was there. I remember sitting at the table in shock. My older sister was the spitting image of my aunt. They talked the same, and had the same mannerisms. My sister could have easily been her daughter. Why did my sister so closely resemble my aunt, when she wasn't raised anywhere near her?

Cindy and Cathy are around their birth mom three or four times a year. Because we have the privilege of knowing her, I can say that my girls not only look like her but they also make some of the same faces she makes, move their hands like she does and so on. They are their mother's daughters.

On the other hand, we have a son who no matter what we do, refuses to work hard. There is no other way to say it—he is lazy. We know from reports that his biological dad refused to work. They told us he was the laziest parent they had ever worked with. We have made our son work, talked about the importance of hard work, and *still* our son refuses to work hard. He is the spitting image of his biological dad, not only in that regard, but also in other ways.

We have a friend who has adopted a few kids, and they have given their kids such wonderful opportunities to succeed. Instead, their adopted son has grown up and he is repeating the exact behavior that he disliked in his birth mom.

Our other friend's daughter is acting just like her birth mom. She goes from guy to guy, whoever will take her, having babies, and now CPS is involved in her life. Her kids will probably all be taken away, just like her moms were. Her biological sister has four kids who have all been taken away as well. Yet, she was taught differently, and given guidance to where she could have lived very differently.

All of my adopted children do things where I think, "I don't have to meet your mom and dad; I'm looking right at them." After raising eight adopted children, I will say, nature is huge. It is bigger than I could have ever imagined.

When taking in these kids, you need to realize that you will be working with genetics and genetics are huge. Mike's uncle has had Mike living with him for a very short time. He knew his biological dad.

He said to me one day on the phone, "I never believed in genetics so much until I got this kid. He is just like his dad."

I said, "I know."

That is not to say that nature will win out, and a child will either be successful or not depending on nature. I also believe that nurture is extremely important, and these children need to be in the most nurturing environment possible.

Don't be quick to disrupt: When we were taking classes to prepare ourselves for foster care, the class was asked to think of behaviors that a child can exhibit that would push your buttons and drive you crazy. One man wrote down that it would drive him crazy if the child left fingerprints on the television. Looking back now, I chuckle at that. Fingerprints on the television would probably be a welcomed behavior if you could talk with him today.

I received a phone call from a lady I had met in class, and she was so upset because the two-year-old in her home wasn't sleeping through the night. She was so tired, and ready to give this child back. She asked me how long I thought it would take before this child slept all night.

The licensing workers and class trainers spend a lot of time trying to prepare you for what you are about to embark on. By the time the child enters your home, you should have been educated enough to know that there will be issues. The kids will be exhibiting all kinds of behaviors that you may or may not be used to. Some of the behaviors they exhibit are normal behaviors, and you may even see the behaviors in your own children. What makes it different is the age of the child exhibiting the behavior, and the duration of the behavior.

Do not take children in if you are going to turn around and disrupt the placement by telling CPS the placement is too difficult. Know it is going to be difficult. Be ready for the long haul. Have your support system in place beforehand. If you have a faith, pray about the placement before it occurs, and have friends and family praying for you. The more disruptions the child has, the more difficult it is for them to heal.

Be prepared to grieve when they leave your home. It is okay to be sad when the child leaves your home. We know when taking the kids in that fostering is temporary and we want them to be reunited with their families if it is at all possible. When and if they do leave, you and your family will be experiencing the loss of the child, but you will also see the child gain his birth family by going back home, or gain a forever family by moving on to adoption. Either way, it can be hard. The foster child can find it difficult as well. They have grown to love you, and they may feel torn about leaving your home. They may even feel guilty about having a hard time leaving your family. You need to give all parties involved permission to grieve. It will affect everyone involved in different ways, and you need to be prepared to be sensitive to any, and all, emotions displayed.

Know your family: You need to know your individual and family strengths and needs. We all have needs, and we have the ability to change those needs into strengths. One example of this is when I shared about embracing a child's culture. This was a need for me. I didn't understand why that was so important. I spent some time taking some classes on that subject to better help myself understand culture, and why it is important to the children in our care. Now, that is a strength for me.

You need to know ahead of time how you are going to support one another. You will also need to make sure, as much as possible, that you have dealt with all the *stuff* in your life that can cause the placement of a foster child to be more difficult.

For example, you cannot go into this thinking a foster child will replace the child you are unable to carry in your womb. He or she will not, and you will end up resenting the foster child in the process. Before taking the child in, you will need to come to terms with the fact that you are unable to conceive a child of your own.

I know someone who had been raped as a child, and they honestly thought they had dealt with it. They had a teenage foster child in their home that acted out once sexually. The acting out was probably a normal behavior for a teenage boy, but they didn't see it that way. Immediately, the foster mom realized there was a serious problem. She saw the child as a predator and from that moment on could hardly look at him, let alone talk to him. At first, she thought it would get better in time. It did not. She eventually had to seek help when she realized the problem wasn't with the foster child—it was with what had happened to her as a child.

If you have things in your past that haven't been dealt with, deal with them before bringing the foster child into your home. Even if you think *the stuff* has been dealt with, be careful. A foster child may come in and do something that might be a trigger for you. That is okay. If that happens, be willing to reach out for help yourself so your past experiences don't affect the child negatively.

Mara

When we entered the shelter to pick up Mike, we realized there was a lot to be desired. I was sharing with my sister-in-law what it was like. She has a get-it-done personality, and she wanted to see what it was like for herself. I explained to her that you have to have permission to enter an emergency shelter. It isn't open for people just to walk through or to visit. She ignored me.

She showed up at the shelter several times. She would knock on the door and ask if she could talk to the person running the shelter. It took a while, but the shelter's supervisor finally got in contact with her. She agreed to meet her at the shelter and talk. The supervisor agreed to let my sister-in-law look around the shelter, and see if there was any way she could help.

My sister-in-law noticed that the place was dark and dreary. The children didn't even have shoes that fit. She was involved with a mom's group at her daughter's school. At the next meeting, she announced a few details regarding the emergency shelter and what she had seen, and they decided to start a shoe drive. That group of mom's sent out a plea for shoes of any size and before long, they had shoes in abundance.

My sister-in-law had every room painted with a theme. The living room housed a giant Winnie-the-Pooh tree and his friends. The hallway was decorated with children handprints and chalkboard paint for notes of who lived in which room. The shelter was filled with furniture, computers, dressers, beds, and linens.

The backyard is now home to a giant wooden play set donated by one of the clients of my sister-in-law's friend, who sent out an e-mail blast to all her clients. We had the company that sells the play set professionally install it. It was paid for by cash donations. With some of the donated money, they purchased TV sets, clothes, and school supplies.

They started celebrating the holidays in a big way! Each child had a birthday cake, singing, games, balloons, and gifts. For Easter, my sister-in-law and her family would start the morning with a pancake breakfast followed by an Easter egg hunt.

Another one of my sister-in-law's friends got her employer to sponsor Christmas for the children in the shelter. It looked like *Toy Land* on Christmas morning. They even had Santa show up Christmas Eve.

Because of her efforts, the children all started school with all the school supplies they needed, plus new school clothes.

They had a backpack drive, so the incoming children would have their own things. When they arrived at the emergency shelter, they had nothing—not even a toothbrush. The emergency shelter was a place they were to stay no more than six days. Some of the children—especially Native American children—may be there for years. This is a true definition of a broken system.

My sister-in-law has since moved on, and has not been to the shelter in a few years, however the momentum has continued.

On one of her many visits, she saw a tiny baby that she fell in love with. She was not called to take in children, but she just loved this child. She wondered why she wasn't in a foster home yet. The reality is there is a shortage of homes. She called us and told us about her. I thought she was crazy. She thought we should consider taking her.

I couldn't stand the thought of a baby in a shelter (as if she was the only one). We began to pray about it. I remember asking my mom if she thought I could care for another baby. She said, "Of course." People used to have children one right after the other. She assured me I would adjust. At this time, we thought Joy and Mike would only be with us about six more months. I knew I could do it for six months.

We called the baby's caseworker and found out that she was born addicted to drugs. Her mom had four other children, all adopted out. Her birth mom gave birth to her, and walked out of the hospital. We are so thankful she gave birth to her in a safe environment, and gave her the opportunity to have a better life. The baby was ten days old.

According to the shelter, because of the drugs she cried for about five hours before falling asleep. She was doing better by day ten. They told us they had notified all known relatives, and none of them were interested in adopting her. In six months they would file abandonment charges on the mother, sever her rights, and the child would be available for adoption. It was an easy case. (Didn't I learn that nothing is easy in the world of foster care and adoption)? They said, "If you want her, she is yours."

It was the day before Thanksgiving. We were busy preparing for our Thanksgiving feast the next day. We decided to take time out of our busy day to go pick up our new little bundle. She didn't have a name, and so we decided to call her Mara. My mom went with me. When we entered the shelter and I got my first look at her, I thought she was awfully tiny. I forgot how small a newborn is. She had a lot of black hair and she was dressed in a pumpkin sleeper. She had the most beautiful light brown complexion. She was the fifth child that came to us with nothing but the clothes on her back.

At first, I thought she had her days and nights mixed up. It ended up for the first week that she slept all day, but all night was waking up for feedings, yet never opening her eyes. I found out it was because she was exhausted from the withdrawals she had gone through. She was such a good baby.

The first week we had her, the other four kids each got the flu. None of them were really old enough to make it to the toilet to throw up. It was a horrible week. I remember trying to adjust to a new baby, and having four other kids—five years old and younger—all sick. But we made it through.

By week three of having Mara, she became very sick. We were at the doctor's office almost daily, because she was having difficulty breathing. On a particular visit, the doctor said he was going to call ahead to Phoenix Children's Hospital and let them know we were on our way. The next week was a blur.

Mara was admitted to the hospital, and ended up being there for eight days. She was one sick baby. They almost admitted her to intensive care, but she managed to dodge that bullet. I stayed with her day and night. Tom stayed with the little ones at home. My mom would get up at four in the morning, drive to the hospital, and let me go home for a shower and rest a little. Around ten, I would return to care for her. It was a difficult time, but also a valuable time. I held Mara on my chest all day and night, and it caused us to bond very quickly.

She was released the evening of Christmas Eve. I made it home in time to see a house full of family. My brother's family had flown in from Florida, and my brother from Iraq, and they were staying with us. My husband had been taking care of them for the past four days while I was in the hospital with Mara. My parents, other brother, and his family were all there to celebrate the holiday.

Looking back now, I don't know how we survived. I was exhausted, Tom was exhausted, the house was a mess, and the festivities hadn't even begun. We made it through, and were looking forward to a little peace and quiet. It had been very stressful since bringing Mara home.

Early on, we realized Mara had asthma. Man was that difficult. At a year and a half, I took her to the doctor and he had her ambulanced from the doctor's office to the hospital for another four-day stay. Less than a year later, she was admitted again for another four days. The asthma would cause pneumonia. I can remember holding her in her hospital bed, and just praying that God would open up her airway and allow her to breathe. It is horrible watching a child struggle to breathe. There were many other times she was very sick with the asthma, but not admitted to the hospital.

She was put on medicine that she took daily to control the asthma, but it still acted up. When she would cough, it would scare me. I never knew what the cough would turn into.

The doctors all called her the happy wheezer. Even when she couldn't breathe, she was happy. The child never stopped running and laughing. She was a child that was going to get after life and nothing was going to stop her.

Mara was such a joy. She was a very happy baby, and so easy to love. Because we were told we would be able to adopt her, we loved her like our own child. We were looking forward to adopting her in the near future. But, with foster care, things don't always turn out like we plan. One thing I have learned: the child in your home is not yours until the judge says the child is. On any given day, any time of day, a relative can step forward and decide they want the child. Even if you have had the child for two years and an adoption date has been set. The family always comes first. They want the child to remain in their biological family if at all possible. Don't ask me why it wasn't that way with Mike though, because I do not know. I think it was just different circumstances.

On May 6, when Mara was six months old, we received a call from her CPS caseworker. She informed us that her supervisor had been looking for Mara's relatives. She found her mother's father, and his current wife. They were told of Mara, and asked if they would be interested in adopting her. They replied that *yes*, they would.

The caseworker was afraid to call me and give me the news, because she knew we would be devastated. We were expecting any day to file for adoption ourselves. She knew they had told us they had contacted all family, nobody was interested, and we could have her. They had made a huge mistake in telling us we could adopt her. We had made a huge mistake in believing them. It was the part of her job she hated, but she had to do it.

We cried and cried and cried some more. We didn't see this one coming. We asked CPS if we could talk to the grandparents. They said they would give them our phone number and if they wanted contact, they would get in touch with us. I remember praying that they would call. I couldn't see myself giving this child to complete strangers. I had given my heart to Mara, and in my heart, she was my daughter.

The grandparents did call and we began talking. We told them all about Mara. We informed them of her hospital stay, and how she was a very sweet, happy, baby. We sent them a package of pictures, and from there—we began the process of waiting. We were told it could take up to six months for all the paperwork to be complete, and for Mara to go live with them in Washington. I knew it would be one of the most difficult six months of my life. I don't think I went a day without kissing that little face and crying, wondering how I would ever hand her over. God was going to have to give me great strength on that day!

Our whole family began the grieving process. This did not only affect Tom and me, it affected all of our children, our parents, and close friends. Cathy was especially close to Mara. She swung her, lay with her on the floor, and laughed with her. They were buddies.

Matt and Ted had a hard time seeing me grieve, and therefore they became angry at the situation. I would explain to them that pain is a part of life, and we would all get through this difficult time.

Four long months passed, and we knew it wouldn't be long before Mara would be leaving. We decided to have our pastor and his wife come over with some close friends. We prayed over Mara that God would protect her and watch over her life as she moved on into a new home. It was September 11. We were meeting with CPS the next day.

The lesson here is that you never know the future when working in foster care and adoption. Nobody knows. The case will probably have many twists and turns, and most of them will catch you off guard. It is important that you remember this and stay focused.

When a relative is located that lives out of state, they have to go through a lengthy process, as did we, to get the child moved into their home. Social Services also wants them to be bonding with the child so that when it is time to move the child, the child is familiar with the one taking them.

CPS told Mara's grandfather that he needed to begin the bonding process. They expected him to come to Phoenix, once a month for a weekend, and take Mara. They would pay for the plane fare as well as the hotel room. Her grandfather informed them that he was too busy with work to make the trip down. Twice, we offered to fly her up there on our dollar, so that they could meet her and she could meet them. We didn't want to hand her over to total strangers. The grandparents said that also would not be possible, because they were just too busy.

CPS was aware of all this, and they became concerned that they were too busy to adopt this child. They informed the grandparents of Mara's existence in May, and it was now September, and they hadn't visited once. They also knew us, and our dedication to Mara. If the grandparents didn't have a free weekend, how were they going to invest the time into her to raise her? But, family always comes first.

We arrived at the meeting on September 12, strangely *my birthday*. Mara's caseworker and caseworker's supervisor were there. At this point, Tom and I were emotionally exhausted, and really just wanted to either have her leave or have her stay. The emotional roller coaster was wearing us down.

We had a conference call with Mara's grandparents, and all of us. They again asked Mara's grandparents what their intentions were with Mara. The grandparents said they planned to adopt her. The supervisor said, "Then you need to come to the next hearing in a couple of weeks, and you need to begin bonding with Mara."

After the phone call was over, the supervisor looked at Tom and me. She said, "You need to hire an attorney, and file a petition to adopt this child."

Talk about confused. I said, "Why? You are going to give her to her grandfather. Why would we waste our time?"

She said, "I can't say, just hire a lawyer, and file a petition to adopt this child."

I thought I was on an emotional roller coaster before. That was nothing to what the next few months would be like.

We came home, and I called an attorney that we know that works with the state. I told him of our conversation, and asked him why she would suggest that I hire a lawyer. He said because they don't want to give Mara to the grandfather, and if we file a petition to adopt her, then the court is forced to look at us as an option for placement. They will then have two possible placements for Mara, and they will look at both and determine which one would be in the best interest of the child.

He gave us the name of an attorney, and we hired him to file the petition.

We attended the next court hearing, as did Mara's grandparents. CPS informed the court that they wanted *us* to adopt Mara, as did our attorney, and Mara's GAL. This did not sit well with the grandparents. It was a very tense hearing.

The grandfather came out of the hearing really angry. His wife looked at him, and I remember her saying, "We need to get to know these people, in case they end up raising Mara."

It was a beautiful day, and so we all decided to sit down outside and talk. I will say it was a little awkward at first.

We went downstairs in the lobby and visited with them for quite a while. Once we all began to relax and be ourselves, we got along very well—and to be honest, they liked us, and we liked them. They knew Mara was bonded with us, and we were the only family she had ever known. They began to feel guilty about wanting to take Mara. Over the next few months, we talked a lot. They went back and forth about whether to take her or not—which was torture.

In December, thirteen months after Mara was born, Mara's biological mom had a baby boy. He had been left at the hospital in the same way Mara was. He was placed into a foster home. The caseworker immediately asked the grandparents if they wanted to take him home. They decided that was what they wanted to do.

The night before the permanency placement hearing, our attorney called Mara's grandparents, and asked them if they would be willing to work out an adoption agreement with us. An agreement where we would be the parents, but the grandparents would have certain rights. They were really scared that once we adopted her, we wouldn't let them see her or be a part of her life. We assured them we would never do that to our daughter, but they wanted an adoption agreement.

I wasn't happy about the terms of the agreement, but at that point, I would have signed anything. It was more like a divorce agreement then a grandparent adoption agreement. We agreed to fly to Seattle once a year so they could see her. They wanted her every other Christmas, and spring break as well as one month out of the summer. We would be responsible to pay all expenses.

When we got to court the next day, it was relayed to the judge that we had come to an agreement. The judge agreed with all parties involved that it would be in the best interest of Mara to stay with us since she was bonded and had been with us since birth.

We were beyond excited that Mara was to be our forever child. It was a miracle. In March of the next year, she was officially given the name Mara Norton. It was one of the best days of our lives.

I will add once the grandparents saw that we had no intention of keeping Mara from them, the adoption agreement changed. Now they live closer, and we see each other whenever it is convenient for both parties. They are really busy with the child that they have adopted, because he has a lot of behavioral issues so Mara doesn't spend any extended days or nights with them.

I will say, I don't advise anyone to get a lawyer and fight for a foster child. We know foster care is temporary, and the case plan is reunification. We would have handed Mara over to her grandparents if all the people involved felt that it was in her best interest. Because CPS did not feel that way, and personally advised us to get a lawyer, we did. I know people who—before parental rights are even terminated—are hiring lawyers to have the child kept with them. Don't do that. Pray and trust God, even when it is tremendously difficult. The child is not yours, and foster care is not adoption.

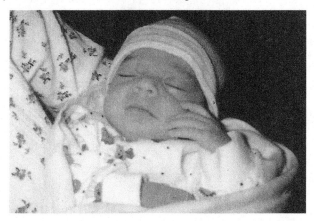

Mara at ten days old

Mara at age nine

Birth family

Most of our children have contact with birth family. We feel it is extremely important that they know where they came from. For the kids that don't have contact with their parents, we have their pictures up with their parent in their room or in their scrapbook. We have even gone online to the Department of Corrections, and gotten a picture of a mug shot of a parent just so the kids can put a name with a face. We know adoptive families that put pictures of family in a shoebox high up in the closet. We don't do that.

We want them to have that connection—even if it is not physical. You can always say to a child that they have their mama's eyes, hair, nose, etc.… That connects them to their biological parent. We made sure that pictures of them with their parents were taken at the visits, just in case severance occurred.

We have had to learn how to set up healthy boundaries with birth families. There was a year when a birth family was in our house for Christmas, and we didn't see any of our own family. That year helped us to realize that we needed to set up some healthier boundaries. We decided that our family came first, and the desires of the birth family would be secondary.

We have had a birth family say to us, "You are now a part of our family." That is very sweet, but not how we see things. The child is a part of our family and the birth family is welcome to visit. We don't have six different families. We have one combined family, with birth connections.

We have a cabin in the mountains that we go to every chance we get. Some birth families have suggested meeting us there for holidays and breaks, but we have yet to invite them or even tell them where our cabin is located. We feel that is our family getaway.

Before sharing each child's individual stories regarding birth family connections, and how we manage them, I want to share a story that is Cathy's, to show how important these connections are.

Cathy came to live with us at thirteen months of age. She has always had her birth mom in her life, which I will share about later. She has always been curious about who her biological father is. She would ask, "When do I get to meet my dad?"

We would ask her mom about her biological father, and she would tell us that he now lives in Mexico, but that she knew his cousin and she would try to get us a picture of him. She never did get Cathy a picture, and Cathy continued to ask. We would always say the same thing. "Cathy, you will never get to meet your dad. He lives in Mexico now. We are so sorry."

When Cathy was almost eleven years of age, her birth mom texted me and informed me that her biological dad was in town, and he wanted to meet her. It just so happened this was on a weekend when Tom had taken the boys on a camping and fishing trip, and I was alone with the girls.

I called a friend who had adopted two children of her own. I explained to her the situation, and that her biological dad was only going to be in town for a few days so I needed to make a quick decision. I asked her what she would do if she was in the same situation. She informed me she would never do it.

I knew how important this was to Cathy. I called her birth mom and asked her if I agreed to have Cathy meet him, would she be able to be there too. She said, "No, that she had to work."

I asked if she thought it would be safe.

She said, "Yes."

I asked if he spoke English.

She said, "No, but he would have an interpreter."

I went back and forth and spent some time praying about it. I finally had a peace that it would be the right thing to do. I called my best friend's husband—who is rather large, and a wrestling coach—and asked him if he would go with us and be our body guard, since I didn't know these people and my husband was out of town. He said he would be happy to do it. I then told Cathy's bi-ological mom that I would give her biological dad one hour of our time. If he was late, I would leave. We made the decision to meet at a public place, and so we picked good old McDonalds.

The next morning, we got up. The girls, my best friend, and I were getting ready for a day of fun. We had a lot of things planned like roller-skating, bowl-ing, and a good girl-flick. After we had eaten breakfast, I pulled Cathy aside and I asked her if she wanted to meet her biological father. Of course she said, "Yes." I explained to her he was in town, and he had asked to meet her.

For the rest of the morning I would say things to her like: "Do you think he is left handed like you? I wonder if he can sing like you can, or if he is good at sports? I wonder if he has tattoos and pierced ears or baggie pants." You get the picture. I wanted to get her thinking about some of those questions.

It was finally time to go. I wasn't nervous up until this point, but I got nervous as we got closer to our destination. Cathy seemed fine; although I'm sure she was a little bit anxious.

We walked into the McDonalds' lobby, and I didn't see anyone but my friend's husband. I asked Cathy to hang out with him while I checked the play-ground area. I walked in the playground area, and saw several Mexicans stand-ing around obviously waiting for someone. A young woman, who I learned was a niece of Cathy's dad, approached me and introduced herself. She was going to be the interpreter for the meeting. She then turned around and intro-duced me to Cathy's dad, his wife, Cathy's little two-year-old half-sister, and a few of Cathy's cousins. There was nothing left to do but for the two of them to finally meet after almost 11 years of waiting and wondering. I thought I was prepared. I was not.

I told them Cathy was waiting for them with her uncle in the lobby of McDonalds. They all followed me into the lobby. Cathy was sitting with her back toward me and as we approached, my friend who was sitting across from Cathy, looked up, which caused Cathy to turn around. I said, "Cathy, this is your dad."

Cathy got up from her seat, turned around, and fell into his arms. Oh my goodness. It was the most beautiful moment I had ever experienced. I still cry about it to this day.

At that exact moment, I had to turn and walk away because I knew I was going to lose it. I did lose it. My best friend came up behind me, put her arm around me, and asked me if I was going to be all right. It took me a few minutes to get myself together, and when I sort of had control, I turned around only to see all the adults crying. It was so amazing!

We all sat down, and they gave Cathy pictures of themselves for her to take home. She found out she had two other siblings living in Mexico. She got to spend some time playing, and getting to know her little half-sister. She asked them questions and vice versa, through the interpreter.

The wife of Cathy's biological dad was extremely emotional. She kissed me several times on the cheek. Through the interpreter, she informed me that her mother died when she was very young. She was raised by someone other than her biological family. She said over and over, "Thank you for taking care of Cathy for us." They were all very thankful for the care Cathy had received, and that she was in a safe and loving environment where she was thriving.

We all took some final pictures of all of them together. We said our good-byes, and then we left.

Cathy carried those pictures around for a few weeks, and showed them to everyone before we eventually put them in her scrapbook.

This was an incredible moment in the life of my daughter, and one that I am sure she will never forget—I know I will never forget it.

I felt like there was something else I wanted her to get out of this meeting, other than just meeting her biological dad. So, I spent some time talking with her about what had just taken place. I asked her if she realized she had just experienced a miracle.

Her biological father got her mother pregnant when they were both very young, and then he left to live in Mexico before Cathy was even born. He was an illegal to our country, and probably would not return to the United States again. It really was not a possibility for the two of them to meet.

I explained to her that God loved her more than she will ever know. God delights in her, and only wants to give her good gifts. He looked down on this great big world with everything there is to see and yet the thing He looked at was her precious little heart. Because He knows her intimately, He knew how important it was to her to know her biological father. God, and only God, caused this special day to happen. I never want her to doubt God's love for her. He loved her so much that He met the desire of her heart.

After that meeting, and it has been a couple of years now, she has never again asked about her dad or where she came from. The curiosity was totally satisfied in the lobby of a McDonalds. Who would have thought?

CINDY AND CATHY

Cindy and Cathy have the same mom, different dads. We met Cindy's dad in court, and gave him a picture of Cindy. He was married with three other children and so he wasn't that interested in Cindy.

When she was initially taken away, he did ask to see her. They had one visit. Cindy was so scared of him she was climbing up the caseworker's back to get away from him. The courts then discontinued any future visits. We do have a picture of him in her scrapbook, and have shown her his mug shot. She understands that it is not safe to have a relationship with him, and that she now has the best daddy in the world.

Right after Cathy met her biological dad, the two girls were both doing a project in school called *All About Me*. The teacher knew that recently Cathy had met her biological dad because she had shown everyone at school the pictures of her meeting with him at McDonalds.

Their teacher caught me one day when I was picking the girls up from school. She wanted to discuss Cindy's *All About Me* story. She informed me that Cindy wrote a story about her and her biological dad. Her story sounded a lot like Cathy's experience meeting her biological father. It was all about a reunion between the two of them, and how wonderful it had been. She wanted to know if Cindy had also met her biological father. I responded that she did not. The teacher then asked if we should make her change her story or leave it like it was. I told her to just leave it. There was no harm in what she had done.

She was jealous of Cathy's meeting with her dad, and she was feeling a void concerning her own biological dad.

That night, my husband decided to sit down with Cindy and have a heart-to-heart talk with her about her biological dad. He was very honest once again about why Cindy could not meet her dad. He explained that God had rescued her from some serious abuse at the hand of her dad, and that God had called him to step in and be the best dad in the world for her. He explained that he would always be there for her, and protect her at all costs.

She sat on his lap, and just cried. My husband held her close, and let her cry until she was finished.

The next day Cindy marched into school, went right up to her teacher, and explained that she wanted to change her *All About Me* story. She made that decision on her own. She explained that she knew the truth about her biological father, and that her original story wasn't true.

When you have several foster or adopted children in your home, you need to be prepared for the experience of one child to possibly affect some of the other children in the home. It may trigger grieving, or nightmares, or any number of issues.

Things have changed since we started this journey. The system now encourages communication between foster parents and biological parents.

When the girls first came to live with us, they had weekly visits with their mom. The system didn't want foster parents to talk with biological parents. We were fortunate enough to have a really neat parent aid (they spend time with the parents, and try to give them parenting tips). She would let us talk with their mom when putting the girls back in the car. Their birth mom would say things like: "I have never seen my girls so happy," or she would comment on how good their hair looked, etc.... I would bring pictures of the girls, and give them to her as well as share things the girls were doing.

Their mom ended up getting pregnant.. She realized she would not be able to care for the girls and a new baby. She asked us if she signed the girls over for adoption, and we adopted them, would we let her have contact with them. We gave her our word that we would never keep the girls from her. She told CPS she wanted to sign over her rights, and soon after, we adopted the girls.

After the adoption took place, we continued meeting with her, usually at McDonalds. She got married, and started settling down. Her mother abandoned her when she was a pre-teen, and her dad worked all the time. She didn't have much direction. Her and her two sisters kind of raised themselves from their early teens. When we would meet, she seemed to enjoy talking with us about her life. My husband tried to give her advice and some direction. I don't think she had any adults in her life that truly cared about her. She became very dear to us.

 After meeting with her for a couple of years, we told her she could start coming to the house. We reminded her that the agreement to see the girls was between her and us. We explained that we didn't feel safe having the girls have contact with any of her extended family. She understood this, and we all agreed.

For years now, she has continued visiting. She has participated in the girls' birthdays, Thanksgiving, Christmas Eve, Mother's Day, she comes over to swim and to just hang out. She sometimes attends the girls' athletic games as well as Christmas programs. I would say she comes three to four times a year. I have the girls call her when significant things have happened in their life, (braces, menstruation, piano recitals, school plays, etc.) so that she feels a part of their lives.

When we have their pictures taken every year, I always get her 5 X 7 pictures of the girls for her collection, so she can enjoy them too. She is so thankful, and I remind her that the two of us have such beautiful, precious daughters to love.

We have gotten some criticism for this relationship. Some people have said she doesn't deserve to see her girls, or that we should never trust her to come to our house. We disagree. She was not fortunate enough to have direction in her life, and so she made some bad choices. That doesn't make her a bad person. She loves her girls, and deserves to know they are safe and loved.

When the girls were little, they would ask why they weren't living with her. I would say, "She was not able to care for you." They would be satisfied with that for a few years, and then they would say:

"Why couldn't she take care of us?"

I would say, "Because she made bad choices." That was good for a while until they wanted to know what bad choices she made. Over the years, we have told them more of their story. We have always been careful to not make their mom out to be a bad person, but to let them know we all make bad choices, and she is worthy of forgiveness.

We have the girls' file. We have pictures of Cindy when she first came into the system—with no hair, and many bruises. There will probably come a day when they will want to read it, and see for themselves. We can only pray that they will be strong enough and healthy enough, to again offer forgiveness and to walk through any hurt feelings they may have. Tom and I will always be there to help them process the abuse.

I have been asked if I am ever jealous of their mom. The answer is *not usually*, but there have been a few times that I've had to remind myself that this is not about me and my feelings. It is about the best interest of the girls. I don't want them to ever wonder where they came from. I don't want them to blame us for keeping them away from their biological mom.

There was a specific day when their biological mom was coming over for a visit, and all day the girls were jumping up and down saying over and over, "Our tummy mom's coming over."

I got sick of hearing it, and wanted to say, "Yeah, what has your tummy mommy ever done for you?" Thank goodness, I have never uttered those thoughts and have been able to put things back into perspective before she arrives. So, yes, I am human, and have had those thoughts from time to time. Thank goodness, I haven't felt that way in years.

Mother's Day was just around the corner, and I was having the girls pick out a Mother's Day card for their mom. She was going to be spending the day with us. One of them picked up a card that was kind of mushy and said, "This one isn't for our tummy mom; it would be for you."

They know who takes care of them. There is no doubt that I am their mom in every sense of the word. They realize the difference between someone giving them birth, and someone caring for them on a daily basis. My relationship with the girls is different from their relationship with their biological mom. But if possible, they should be given the opportunity to love both. What a gift that is for our kids.

Their biological mom always calls me on Mother's Day. She comments that her girls have turned into beautiful, talented girls, and that she couldn't have given them the life they have now. When they play the piano for her, she breaks down and cries. She is quick to thank us for taking such good care of them. I remind her that the girls are so blessed to have two mommies that love them very much.

We truly love her, and we know she loves us. We look forward to sharing many more years sharing our girls with her. We hope our girls continue to grow in their relationship with her as they move into adulthood. We think this is the healthiest way to raise them.

DAVID

David came to live with us when he was eleven. He had lived with his birth mom and step dad before being taken away. His mom was a drug and alcohol user. When he was taken away, he went to live with his grandma and grandpa. His aunt and her four children were also a huge part of David's life.

David's grandparents were in very poor health. They loved David, and wanted to take care of him, but they knew they could not give him what he needed. His aunt was asked to take David, but she had four children of her own and didn't know how she could take another one.

When David came to live with us, he would visit his grandparents once or twice a month. We would drop him off, and pick him up usually the next day. One day when I dropped him off, I noticed an unusual car parked in front of their house. I went in the house, and David's biological mom was there.

Our agreement for visits with David was between *David and his grandparents*, not his biological mom, and the grandparents were aware of this. They thought they could sneak David's mom over, and we wouldn't realize it.

This is something you have to be ready for. Blood is thick. A lot of families will lie to you. They will try to sneak other family members in for a visit that you have not agreed to. I know family members want to see the child, but it is our job as parents to not only protect our children physically, but also emotionally.

We were all standing in the kitchen together. I felt like I was stuck between a rock and a hard place. It was a tad bit awkward to say the least. I decided to walk up to his biological mom, and introduced myself. We had some small talk and after a while, it was time for me to leave. I was reluctant to leave David there. I didn't really know what I should do.

I took David aside and asked him if he would be comfortable if I left. He said he would be okay. I decided that I wasn't going to leave him for the night, because his biological mom had a strange looking guy there with her, and I just wasn't comfortable with the whole thing.

I returned a few hours later to get him. I was standing on the porch with David's grandparents, his biological mom, and his aunt and her kids who had also come over for a visit. His biological mom informed me that she thought he looked skinny, and asked me if I was feeding him enough. I assured her I was. (I held my tongue...I wanted to say something like...Are you kidding me? When we got him he had 11 cavities, was over a hundred pounds overweight, and had been horribly abused—and you have the nerve to ask if I feed him?) Thank goodness, I watched my words. This was one time where it was hard to keep my mouth shut.

His biological mom then proceeded to follow David and me out to the car. I was getting ready to pull out of the driveway, when she began to bang on the window. I was a little startled. I rolled my window down, and politely asked her what she needed. She began to cry. She wanted me to know that she loved David, but that she just couldn't take care of him. I told her I understood that and we were happy to take care of him for her. She continued to make quite a scene, and I noticed David sitting with his head down. Finally, I said I needed to go. I began backing the vehicle out of the driveway while rolling up the window at the same time. She was left standing in the driveway looking at us leave.

At that moment, I felt so sorry for David. I felt I hadn't protected him from the emotional turmoil of seeing his biological mom, and watching her behavior. He had already been through so much! I didn't want him to suffer more at the hand of his biological mother.

I have never lied to the kids, nor will I. I know sometimes what they have to hear can be difficult for them, but necessary. I knew that I needed to take the time driving home to talk with David about what had just happened.

I first apologized to David, then I told him I should have been smarter regarding the visit. We proceeded to talk about his biological mom.

I said, "You know your mother could take care of you, if she made better choices?"

He said, "Yes," that he knew that. I then explained to him how we don't live in a bubble, and how our choices affect so many others in our lives. Sometimes, we don't think one little decision can be all that important. But one little decision usually leads to another little decision until you are on either a path that will cause you and others harm, or a path that will be beneficial to you and those around you.

It has been hard for David. When he had been with us for only four years, his grandparents both died within a month of each other. They were so special to David, more like parents then grandparents. When he went over to their house for a visit, he would help them clean their house and yard. In the last two years of their lives, he was helping take care of them. It was extremely emotional for him to watch them fail in health. It really was a lot for a 13-year-old boy to handle.

When the death of David's grandpa was getting close, his biological mom showed up once again to be with the family. During this time, his mother would once again promise that she was going to get off drugs and clean herself up. She told David she was going to start to be around to interact with the family. It was all the things addicts tell their loved ones. David told me this, and I could see the excitement and hope in his eyes. I knew he believed her. I never said anything to discourage his hope. He would be disappointed soon enough.

Since his grandparents died, he has not seen his mom. That was over a year ago.

David also has a relationship with his aunt and cousins. Throughout the year, he goes over to visit, and he also attends his cousins' birthday parties. During the summer, we leave town and David likes to attend workouts with his football team. We asked his aunt if she would keep him for the summer. So, he spends about six weeks with them every summer. They are a sweet family, and so far they have been respectful of us and the boundaries we have set up regarding his biological mom.

His aunt did say to him once that she wishes she would have taken him into her home. I didn't think that was an appropriate thing to say to a child since all children wish they lived with their birth family. I asked him if he wished he lived with her and he said, "No." He realizes if he had gone with her, he would probably still be 100 pounds overweight, and not playing any sports. He said he also likes having a mom, dad, and still an aunt. I thought that was pretty perceptive for a 15-year-old. Whether he really feels that way or not, I'm not sure.

David has several siblings. He has a younger brother and sister that have been adopted and live about two miles from us. The family is wonderful, and whenever David wants to see them, they have him over for the day.

He has twin sisters that were adopted by another family. We got together with them one time when we first got David. He hasn't seen them since. He hasn't asked.

We don't know where his birth father is. He also has an older brother whom he has no contact with.

I made the mistake of being the one to make sure my adopted kids see their birth connections. But, it was a lot of work, and I realized the kids weren't asking to see them before I was making plans to get together. I do it differently now. I don't mention birth family visits. I wait for my kids to request a visit. I let the older children make the phone call, and set up the arrangements to get together with them.

Joy

Our sweet little Joy, I feel sorry for her. Her biological mom and dad were not healthy, and we knew it would not be safe for her to continue contact with them. She has two half-brothers who were adopted by another family. We were given that information, and we contacted the adoptive family. They didn't believe in birth family connections, and wanted nothing to do with Joy. They felt that her brothers needed a new start without anyone from their past. After we had Joy for 9 years, I tried again to contact them to see if their feelings toward birth siblings had changed. Once again, they refused to meet Joy, and I'm sure they won't even mention my phone call to the boys. I keep the information regarding the boys in a file. When they turn 18, I will look for them. They were older when they were adopted and so they will remember Joy. They are probably wondering what happened to her.

PAUL AND SARAH

Paul and Sarah's dad is in prison and their mom is mentally ill. They have a brother who was adopted out at the age of 17. They also have an older sister who wanted nothing to do with adoption, so she lived in a group home until she aged out of the system at age 18.

Their sister met a guy and they moved in together. She had a baby and from what I've heard, she has had another one since. She now shows up at our door, unannounced, about once a year.

When Paul and Sarah first came to live with us, we would go get their sister from the group home and she would come over for a visit. She was not happy that they were going to be adopted. She has always had a chip on her shoulder—which is understandable—for all she has been through. When she does show up, we never leave the kids alone with her. We don't feel safe or comfortable about the influence she may have on them. When they grow up, they will probably find each other (we don't have her phone number, because she constantly changes it) and hopefully they will be able to form a healthy relationship with her.

Their brother shows up about once a year as well. He joined the military, and is trying hard to lead a productive life. Because he is older, the kids hang on every word he says. We stay close so we can listen to the conversation, and make sure it is appropriate. It is so important that we keep these kids safe—physically as well as emotionally. That can be hard if birth family is filling their head with negativity.

MARA

You may remember that Mara came to live with us when she was a mere ten days old. We are the only parents she has ever known. I find it interesting that she has made up stories about her *tummy mommy* since she was old enough to talk.

One night when Mara was probably about five years old, I decided to take the kids out to Baskin Robbins Ice Cream. We all got out of the car, and that is where her story began. She became extremely excited as she began to tell all of us that she had been at this Baskin Robbins before with her tummy mommy. She then proceeded to tell us that they were both wearing their pajamas at the time. Her mommy had hair down to her ankles, and she had to be careful the ice cream didn't get in her hair. She was holding Mara in her arms, because

Mara forgot her slippers. When we entered the parlor, she showed us all what kind of ice cream they each had.

There have been many occasion where we are walking into a store, or going to a park, and she will start in with a story about her and her biological mom being there once before. She is very descriptive. She always tells me what they were wearing, what their hair looked like, and what they bought or did. It is really kind of cute.

I never burst her bubble. I let her dream, because for some reason it is important to her. She knows her biological mom gave birth to her, and left the hospital so she would have a better life. She knows she has never lived with her mom. She knows her mom has been in jail. Yet, she continues to make up fantasies about her. It's all good.

During one of her stories, I heard one of the boys say to her, "That's not true. Your mom abandoned you at the hospital when you were born."

I was quick to jump in. I never tell my kids they were abandoned. Instead I say, "Your mommy loved you so much, and she knew she couldn't take care of you. She went into the hospital, gave birth to you, and gave you the opportunity to have a better life. We are forever grateful for the choice she made to give you life."

We want their adoption to be a beautiful thing, not a negative thing. After all, her mom could have had her in a crack house, kept her, and not taken care of her. We truly are thankful for the choice she made to walk out after Mara was born. It had to be a difficult choice for her.

I did get pictures of her mom from her grandfather, and they are in her scrapbook along with pictures of two of her siblings. The last time her mom got out of jail, Mara's grandfather gave me her mom's phone number. I have never had a peace about calling her. Mara's biological mom hasn't been healthy in years, and continues to be in and out of jail. I don't think it would satisfy Mara to meet her. I think Mara would want to see her on a regular basis, and I don't feel that her mom has the ability to do that at this time.

Mara's grandpa keeps us updated, and maybe someday that will be possible, but not now. Always consider the best interest of the child. Just because one child is meeting a birth relative, doesn't mean it will be healthy for another child to do the same. Think it through, and pray a lot.

One year after Mara was born, her biological mom gave birth to another child. Mara's grandpa and his wife took that child in. When we first adopted Mara, her grandparents lived in Washington. We took a trip there twice for a visit and they came here one year for Christmas. They have since moved to Prescott where they spend the winter months. We get together periodically with them, so she can know her half-brother and her grandparents. It is funny how excited she gets when we spend the day with them.

MIKE

Mike was taken away from his parents because of abuse and failure to protect. His mom was not married to his dad, but she refused to leave him—even though he was living with Joy's mom. We didn't feel Mike's mother would actually be a threat herself if we allowed her to see Mike. We chose not to allow visits between the two of them, because Mike's father was a very violent man, and we knew we could not trust Mike's biological mom not to tell the dad when and where we would be meeting. We had to cut all ties with his parents. Soon after he was adopted, his mom passed away from diabetes.

Shortly after we adopted Mike, CPS contacted us and said it was totally up to us, but that Mike's grandma and uncle on his mother's side would like to meet us. CPS informed us that they were really sweet people. We thought and prayed about it, and decided that we should go for it.

We set up a meeting at a restaurant around the corner. We did not take Mike with us. We wanted to first get a feel for them ourselves. We met for lunch, and we had a nice visit. It was hard on Mike's grandma. Her daughter, Mike's biological mom, had passed away—and Mike was all she had left of her daughter. She was pretty emotional talking about it. We assured her that she was welcome to be a part of Mike's life, as much or as little, as she wanted. She lived in Nevada, but she came to the Phoenix area quite often to visit family.

A few months after that meeting, we received word from her that she would like to come and visit Mike. She wanted to bring her other son who lived in California. She wanted him to also meet us. They were going to be in Phoenix for three days. We put those dates aside, so that when they got here we could spend all the time with them.

They attended church with us, and afterwards we went for a picnic in the park. We all watched a movie with the kids later that day. The next day, we went to the zoo together and had a fabulous time getting to know each other better. We took all the kids out for dinner, and they came to the house and played on the trampoline with the kids.

After that visit, we continued to have a relationship with them. They would come into town once or twice a year, and they always made it a point to stop in and see Mike. Mike looks and acts a lot like his uncle so it was good for him.

It is not always a healthy situation to meet with birth family. It is okay to agree not to meet, but to give the information to the kids so when they are old enough they can make the decision of getting together with birth family themselves.

One of my friends gets together with her girl's birth family once a year. It is always a disaster. The older brother takes control. He molested all the girls, which brings up bad memories and makes it difficult for everyone. The kids don't talk to each other; they just stare at the TV. Everyone leaves upset. I don't feel a visit like that is beneficial emotionally, and so therefore, I wouldn't have it.

In a situation like that, I would just have pictures of them all together for them to see until they were older and could choose on their own.

I have a good friend that has adopted three kids. We swap stories on a regular basis, and it helps us laugh at the difficult. She recently told me a story about her 14-year-old daughter. Her daughter was at dance class, and the kids decided to get together and talk about the worst thing that has happened to them in their life.

Her daughter did not mention living under a bridge, watching horrific abuse between her father and mother, never going to school, not having enough food to eat and so on. She instead mentions the fact that she was adopted.

When my friend, her adoptive mother, heard this—she was so hurt. She couldn't believe that her daughter, whom she had had since she was six years old, mentioned the adoption like it was a bad thing. Her initial thought was to scream at her, then throw her out back with some bread and water, and throw her a blanket and pillow so she could sleep under the patio cover.

Instead, she called me and we talked. It is hurtful, and yet our minds get it even when our hearts don't. Her daughter loves her new family; there is no doubt about that. Her daughter is thriving in her adopted home, and has so much opportunity now. The reality of it though is that these children would rather, no matter what the circumstances, be with their biological family if they had the choice.

Her other daughter, who is now 18, decided to write a letter to her father in prison. Her therapist thought this would be a great idea. Her adoptive mom asked her what she hopes to gain from writing the letter. Her response was that she wanted to receive an apology from her father. She also was hoping that he would agree to have a relationship with her once he was out of prison. You know, fireworks, that sort of thing. The father did respond to her, and the correspondence between them has continued.

There have been times my friend has called me sobbing. Her two girls will get a letter from their birth father, and nothing else in the world matters but the words on the page. She wants to scream, "What are you writing about? Are you thanking him for beating and raping all of you?"

She feels she has invested a lot of time and energy into the kids getting them healthy, and they don't care. She knows if the birth parent showed up, the kids would most likely run off to their birth parent. She sometimes wonders if they realize all she has done for them, and the sacrifices she has made.

She doesn't get it—and yet she does. It can be very hurtful. You have to keep control of your emotions so you don't say something you can never take back. It is shocking to hear, and yet we know that will always be these kids' desire. They don't understand why their parents are incapable of a healthy relationship with them. It can be hard to watch our children reach out, knowing they will most likely get hurt once again.

Hopefully, when these kids get older, and their minds are capable of understanding the bigger picture, they will realize who has been the constant in their life. Hopefully, they won't be so quick to move into an unhealthy relationship with their birth families that will cause them to get hurt.

One of the hardest things not to do, is bad-mouth their biological family. Let's face it. Their biological family has been less than perfect, and has probably done some horrible things to their kids. It is easy to want to say, "Your dad's a loser," or "If your mom really loved you, she would have left your dad." Stuff like that. Don't do it. Those thoughts are going to run through your mind, because you are human. Don't let them come out of your mouth.

The kids are a part of their parents. When you bad-mouth their parents, you are in essence bad-mouthing who they are. The outcome of that is not good. Keep your negative thoughts to yourself—or between you and a trusted friend. Better yet, pray for their parents that the cycle of abuse would stop with them.

It is also important that you forgive their parents for the abuse and neglect that they subjected their child to. You can then, in turn, help the child with the issue of forgiveness they may have. We don't want these children to harbor a lack of forgiveness in their hearts. It will then turn into bitterness that will affect their life for years to come. We want these kids to be healthy.

After adopting eight children, I believe we all have a God-given desire to know where we came from, and to feel wanted and loved by those people. I have seen it over and over again in my kids. They have a deep desire to keep these connections open.

I wish that all adopted parents would put their personal feelings aside, and think of the best interest of the children. These children did not choose to get ripped out of the only family they knew—healthy or not. They didn't choose to lose contact with the people they love. We don't want them to have feelings of abandonment, and wonder if something is wrong with them.

Some adoptive parents feel that if the birth parents or family is still involved, it will hurt their child's ability to fully bond with them. They also feel threatened by the birth family. As humans, we are all able to love more than one person. I was sharing with a teacher one day that the girls' birth mom was coming over for a visit. The teacher replied, "Doesn't that confuse the girls?"

I said, "No, they can count. They know they have two moms."

Above: David with two younger siblings, his aunt and four cousins.
Below: Cindy and Cathy with their birth mom

Above: Mara with her grandparents and half-brother

Below: Cathy's biological father and half-sister

Above: Paul and Sarah with their two siblings
Below: Mike's uncle and grandma

Paul and Sarah

After Mara, we really thought we were done bringing children into our home. It had been a long five years with a lot of work and heartache. It had been three years since adopting any children, and we were content with that. The kids were all growing beautifully and they were keeping us busy.

As time went on, I knew in my heart that God wasn't done using us in this capacity. I thought I was crazy, so I didn't say anything to Tom. When Tom and I were driving to California alone to celebrate our twenty-fifth wedding anniversary, the subject was brought up by him. I guess he also knew God wasn't done with us yet either.

We talked about what it would mean to bring in more children. I remember specifically asking *how on earth* I would have the strength to do more. He responded with, "Jill, if God is calling us to take in more children, he won't give us the strength until we obey him, and those kids are stepping across our doorstep and into our house." I knew he was right. But I didn't know if I wanted to obey.

Some time went by, and on a day in December, we received a call from our caseworker regarding two children. One was a nine-year-old girl, and her brother was thirteen. They were in a foster home with an elderly lady who had been doing foster care for years. She was now 75 years old, and ready to retire. Her license was about to expire. If they didn't find a home for these two kids within the week, they would be put into separate group homes.

We were told if we were interested, to call the foster mom and get some details regarding the children. Well, to be honest I didn't want a thirteen-year-old boy. We all have heard the stories about the thirteen-year-old foster kids. Almost nobody takes thirteen-year-old foster kids, especially boys, and there is a reason for that. I had five other little kids in my home to consider. God

couldn't possibly be asking me to take these two kids in. I really wasn't interested.

To make everyone happy, I called the foster mom and got some information regarding the siblings. Of course, I heard the words, "They have no
behavioral issues whatsoever." Why do we fall for that? She explained to me
that they had been living with her for almost a year. She said they were really
good kids. I found it a little strange that when I asked what the little girl's name
was, she couldn't even tell me. I asked her to spell it, and she had a problem
with that as well. Oh my!

In the next few pages I am going to share with you what we said to each
other and how we felt. It is not politically correct, and may be offensive. I will
apologize ahead of time if that is the case. I just want to be real.

It was a Monday, and Paul and Sarah were going to be put into a group
home on Saturday. Tom and I felt like we should at least go meet with them.

We got the information we needed, and headed off to their current foster
home. When we arrived, we sat down with the foster mom, Paul and Sarah.

Sarah was a fat little thing. She wore clothes about two sizes too small,
and they made her look like a boy. Her hair was cut very short, and was un-
kempt, but combed. When she spoke, we realized she had a speech problem.
She spoke with her hands—which was cute. She had an odd look about her.

She was the more talkative of the two, and so we began finding out a little
information about her. She told us she liked school, and did very well in her
studies. We showed her pictures of our family, and told her a little bit about
the kids. We asked her if they attended church. She replied that she and Paul
walked to the little Baptist church down the street every Sunday to attend
services. She then commented that she didn't know how to pray, and that she
wished someone would teach her how to pray.

Paul was sitting across from us in a chair. We noticed that he never made
eye contact. He also had a different look about him. He was holding a basketball and was smiling, but not at anyone in particular. I found this Pecu-
liar. When we were talking with Sarah, Paul would interrupt us frequently.
He would say, "You want to know a fact?" We realized he also had a speech
problem.

We would reply, "Sure." He would then rattle off some fact about a whale. A few minutes later, he would repeat the process.

"You want to know a fact?"

We would again say, "Sure." He would tell us another fact. That was the entire conversation with Paul. I really felt sorry for both of them. They seemed like lost little children.

We got done visiting with them, and let them know we would talk it over with our family and get back with them. *How awful is that for a kid?* I can't even imagine what it is like for an older child to be a *foster* child, and be so displaced.

We got in the car quite relieved that it was over, and the first words out of my husband's mouth were, "I'm not taking those kids, that boy is retarded." I agreed that there was obviously something wrong, and I wasn't interested either. Someone else would have to step up and care for the two of them.

We went home, quite certain that those two children would not be entering our home. We got on with our lives.

I believe it was Thursday of the same week, I was driving myself to the dentist when I heard the Lord speak to my heart. No, not audibly. I could sense Him in my spirit.

He said as clear as day, "Jill, I want you to bring those two children into your home."

I said, "No, Lord. I agreed to give children a home, and I have done that. But, I am not going to raise a retarded child. That is over and above anything I have agreed to do." I felt like he would understand. After all, that didn't sound unreasonable to me. I was sure God would agree with me.

A few minutes later, my spirit once again spoke. I heard very clearly, "He is not retarded, he is fearfully and wonderfully made, and I want you to go get him."

I couldn't possibly be hearing correctly. Please, don't ask this of me, I thought. I then started crying. I did not, and I mean *did not*, want to go get him. I cried, and really begged God not to ask that of me. I felt like it would be too much. I decided to bargain with God. He knew that Tom and I never tried to convince each other to bring in any children. If it was truly God's will, then God was going to have to convince Tom of that. If Tom said we had to do it, then I would agree. But you can bet I wasn't about to say one word. I got my teeth cleaned, and headed home hoping that Tom wasn't going to hear from God anytime soon. And if he did, I was hoping for the first time in our lives together that my husband wouldn't listen, and certainly would not obey.

Friday morning we got up and went about our business as usual. I was in the kitchen preparing breakfast for the other children. Tom was preparing for a day at work. We talked for a while before he walked out the door to leave for work. "Whew, I thought. Nothing was mentioned regarding the children. I think I am off the hook."

Oh No! I heard the front door reopen. My husband enters the kitchen and looks directly into my eyes. He said, and I will never forget his words, "Honey, who is going to teach that little girl how to pray?"

I replied, "We are."

He said, "Make the phone call, so we can go pick up those kids."

In my heart, I already knew God was going to win. I was resigned to that, but I was not particularly happy about it.

Before bringing any new kids into the home, we would always talk to the other kids in the home about it first. We would tell them a little bit about the kids that needed a home, and then we would take a family vote.

We think it is fair for all people involved to have a say in the situation. After all, it can affect the birth order of some of the other children. A child that was the youngest may not be the youngest anymore. They may or may not like that. Sarah was the youngest in her family, but if she came to live with us, she would instantly have four younger siblings. Her position as baby of the family was shifted. It affects all the children, and it is an adjustment on everyone, not only on Tom and me.

With that being said, if even one child was against bringing in more children, then we wouldn't do it. Everyone has to be on board, or it won't work.

In this instance, everyone voted to open up our hearts and home to two more children in need of a family.

We called the kids' caseworker, and informed them that we would be HAP-PY to bring the kids into our home. They asked us to pick them up on Saturday.

Saturday came, and we headed over to get them and their belongings. When we had visited with the children earlier in the week, they showed sadness over the fact that they would be leaving. They loved their foster mom, and even called her Grandma. We wondered how it would be for them leaving. I asked the foster grandma if she had any pictures of them over the last year, so I could put them up in their room. But she did not.

We noticed that as we were packing up the van, the foster grandma asked Paul what he thought he was doing. She noticed a lot of stuff in his belongings that were not his. She scolding him for taking some PlayStation games and equipment, and then told him to go put it back in her house. We thought at the time that it was a misunderstanding.

We assured the kids that they would be able to visit their foster grandma any time they wanted, and that they were not saying good-bye for good. We exchanged phone numbers, and she communicated to the kids that she wanted to hear from them on a regular basis. They hugged, and then we were ready to go.

We had a babysitter for all the other kids, so we then headed to the store for clothes. The kids would be starting at the private school on Monday, and they would need uniforms along with clothes that fit. We spent a few hours getting them everything they would need.

We arrived home. As we pulled up to the house, I was wondering if what Tom had said to me a few months earlier was true. Remember, he had said that when we obeyed God, and not a moment before, God would give us the strength needed to complete the task before us. I was holding on to that promise, because I was feeling a bit overwhelmed.

We introduced all the kids to each other and showed them to their new room. Everyone seemed to be excited to have two new members added to the family.

I can remember a thought I had the first day Paul was with us. He was using the bathroom, and he plugged up the toilet. We had to use a plunger, and I remember seeing the embarrassment on his face as we were fixing the problem. We were total strangers to him.

If you are in your own home and you plug up the toilet, no big deal. You plunge it. What if you plug up a complete stranger's toilet? You would be totally embarrassed. I remember, at that moment, feeling such empathy for these kids. How hard it must be for them to be thrust into a situation that is really uncomfortable, and probably a little scary.

We got everyone settled, and seemed to get into a routine relatively quickly. I registered them in school, and got all their school supplies. I introduced them to the teachers, and off we went.

I remember my son Ted saying to me, "Boy Mom, you are getting good at this."

I said, "You think so? Why?"

He replied, "This is the first set of kids you've gotten that you didn't just sit down and sob." I thought, how perceptive of him. He was right. By kid number six and seven, I was used to what was happening, and I didn't panic. I was getting good at this.

We had Paul for about two weeks, when one of my friends came over to meet the new kids. She works with kids with disabilities and is very knowledgeable. She was in my house for about ten minutes watching Paul continue to come into the kitchen to share facts with me.

She said, "Jill, he has Asperger's."

I said, "What is that?"

She then explained to me that it is a form of autism. They focus on one thing, and Paul's one thing was facts. She told me to get him evaluated.

I called his old foster mom, and asked her if she realized something was wrong with Paul. She said that "Yes, she did." She told me she had taken him to a doctor, but they couldn't find anything wrong with him. I asked her if she took him to a medical doctor or a psychologist. She said medical doctor. I knew that is why he wasn't diagnosed. I couldn't believe he was thirteen years old, and nobody had ever gotten him any help.

So, I took him to a well-known psychologist. He had Paul evaluated and sure enough he had Asperger's. When he was asked to draw a picture of his family, he drew a picture of three crosses on a hill. The psychologist asked him where the people were. He replied, "Oh, you wanted people in the picture?"

We began to learn a lot about his disorder. We found out that people with Asperger's are socially retarded. We also learned that he can be taught social skills. The social skills will never be easy for him, but he can learn how to communicate appropriately.

We noticed when someone would come to the door—he would open it, but not say a word. I would say, "Paul, say hello and ask them to please come in." He would do that, but it was very awkward. He has a very difficult time making eye contact with other people.

When picking him up from school, I would ask him how his day was and he would reply, "AWESOME." I would ask him why it was awesome, and he could not answer the question. I would notice that he would comment on a commercial or something someone said, and his comment would not make any sense. He didn't understand things a child his age shouldn't have any trouble understanding.

He is an amazing artist, and he was able to complete his schoolwork although he is extremely slow at all tasks. When we finally had him evaluated for special needs classes, we were told that he is able to look at a textbook and answer specific questions from that text. That is why he is able to complete his schoolwork without too much trouble.

When he reads, he comprehends on the level of a fifth grader and that will not change. He also has difficulty writing. He cannot put thoughts into words, because his thoughts don't really make a lot of sense. I love when he asks me to edit one of his papers. I read it, and not a word makes sense. It is horrible. If I edited it for him, it would change every word on every page—and I'm not sure that would be a benefit for him. I try to give him ideas so that he can write, and someone could semi-understand what he is trying to convey.

Shortly after he came to live with us, we sent him off to church summer camp. I was nervous because I knew he was very "odd." I also knew he didn't know anybody, but that didn't seem to bother him. I worried about him the whole time he was gone, and I prayed every day that he would make a friend or two. When he got home, I asked him how it went and he said it was "AWE-SOME." I asked him if he made any friends, and his response was, "Yes, I met 256 friends."

I said, "Do any of them have a name?" He gave me a blank stare like he couldn't figure out why I was asking for a name. It didn't take long for me to realize that Paul doesn't have a friend in the world except us. He is very much a loner.

When Sarah first arrived, it was precious. She had never had someone fix her hair. She thought it was cute seeing herself in little pigtails or a French braid. We bought her some dresses and dress shoes for church. She put a beautiful pink and green sun dress on, and just stared at herself in the mirror. She informed me that she had never worn a dress before, and she felt like a princess. When she came downstairs, Paul couldn't believe his eyes. He was so happy to see her dressed up. She was also not used to girl's clothes or clothes that even fit for that matter. It was a new experience for her.

I remember the first shower she took. She couldn't stop talking about how good the water felt. She told me when living with her birth family, they had to take cold showers.

When their two siblings were over for a visit, we heard all about the trailer they lived in with their mom. It had no door and no windows whatsoever. They used the stove for heat, and they all slept together on the floor.

The older kids don't usually sit down and tell you their life story. You will get bits and pieces of it as time goes on. Some of the things you hear can be a little shocking, and it can be difficult not to react, and say something negative. Here is an example:

One time we had sugar pops cereal as an option for breakfast. She informed me that she hated sugar pops, because one time her dad put beer in her cereal bowl instead of milk—and all she remembers is throwing up all morning because of it. I told her she could eat something else. I wondered to myself, "Who does stuff like that?"

Time went on, and we began to notice certain behaviors from Paul and Sarah that were not *normal*. I will start with the behaviors that Paul exhibited first.

Paul would steal food constantly. I would find a backpack in his room full of boxes of food. He wouldn't take one granola bar; he would take the whole box. When I would find it, he would of course lie about it. He would tell me the boxes were from before he came to live with us.

When he would come out of church, I noticed that every pocket on his body was shoved full of food. I explained to him that the food was there for him to eat while attending church. It wasn't for the following week. I would make him go back into the Sunday school class, and put the food back. We had food at home he could have. He didn't need to stockpile it.

In the beginning, I asked them questions about this. I knew they had been in the other foster home for almost a year, and they were fed well there. I asked them if they were fed when living with their mom and grandma.

They replied that yes, they were fed three meals a day. I asked them if they were good meals and they both said that, yes, it was food like what I fixed. I couldn't figure out why they felt the need to hoard and steal food. It got so bad, that we put locks on the cabinets so they couldn't get to the food. Paul seemed to improve as time went on, although he also improved in his ability to sneak. I'm not sure to this day, if he still takes food or not.

Another behavior that he exhibited was he was afraid to give me his dirty clothes. I do the laundry every day, and I began to notice that I never had any dirty clothes from him. When I asked him about it, he would assure me that he had put them in the laundry basket. I would inform him that they weren't there. He would get really nervous, and so I began searching his room. This would make him crazy. He would try to stop me, but I just kept looking around. Eventually, I would find his dirty clothes between the mattresses or under his bed, behind his pillow or anywhere, but in the laundry.

It reminded me a lot of Cindy when she was afraid for me to leave the house and we had to set the timer for her. It is a trust issue. My dad told me to just let him hide his clothes. He didn't understand why I couldn't just let these kids have their crazy issues. I reminded my dad that is not the way to teach trust.

I explained to Paul that I was going to take his clothes, wash them and give them back to him that same day. He would come home from school to find his clothes folded neatly and lying on his bed. We went through this ritual for several weeks until finally he learned that I would wash his clothes and give them back to him. It was a happy day when I found his clothes in the laundry room, and not under his mattress. It saved me some time from having to hunt them down.

Paul also had a terrible problem with stealing. One day, I found a backpack in his room full of wrestling equipment. He didn't need the equipment. He wasn't even on the wrestling team, but felt he should take it from the locker room at school anyway. When I found it, I made him take the equipment back to school and explain to the coach that he had taken it, and it wasn't his. I also told him I would be calling the coach to make sure he returned it.

On another occasion, I found shaving cream (he wasn't shaving), deodorant (he had his own), and someone else's shorts hidden in his backpack. Once again, I explained that those items didn't belong to him, and it was stealing. I don't care where he found them, they weren't his, and he had no right to take them. Please return them and stop this madness!

I would catch him going through the lost and found items at the aquatic center when we went there to swim. He would come out with a handful of things that were not his. Again, this is stealing. Is it yours? If not, you have no right to take it. It is stealing.

It has not stopped. We continue to find things missing around the house. Some of the things he steals just don't make any sense. Tom's Cardinals shirt, a phone charger that doesn't go with his phone, and a phone are some of the things that he has taken. We really began to feel like we had a stranger in the house.

He was extremely sneaky, and it would make us very uncomfortable.

To this day, things continue to disappear and it is hard to not suspect him. He will be moving out soon, and we are hoping that stops the disappearing act.

One spring, my husband planted a garden in the back yard. He loves to garden, and was looking forward to a few fresh vegetables on his plate. One Saturday morning we were all doing chores around the house. I walked out back only to find that Paul had unplanted all the plants, and was putting them in buckets.

He was then going to re-dig up the yard, and re plant them. I was a little taken back at the sight of my husband's garden all pulled up. I asked Paul what he was doing. He informed me that he didn't like the way Dad planted the garden, and so he was going to do it differently. He was 18 years old at the time of this event.

I said, "That is so sweet of you, but you can't do that. You just killed all the plants." He just stared at me, and I think we were both in disbelief. I told him that in the future, he needed to ask before taking on big projects all on his own.

My husband didn't let him know how upset he was. He stewed in private—after all, there was nothing we could do about it. We didn't want him to feel bad, or demean him. We understand that he has a disability, and that he doesn't think like the average person.

One day my husband asked him to help him get the boat motor out of the back of the truck. My husband instructed Paul to take it out, and set it upright just like it was sitting in the truck. Tom told me he turned around to see Paul trying to turn it upside down with the propeller sticking straight up in the air. We just cracked up!

My husband had to go out of town for three days, and so I was alone with the kids. It was a Sunday, and we were really busy. We went to church, got groceries, and we had to take Cathy to a friend's birthday party, and so on.

I was running around like a chicken with its head cut off, and I noticed something rather odd. Apparently, Paul decided to clean the fish tank. While cleaning the tank, he put the fish in a bucket with only a little water. When I walked into the room I noticed a few fish missing, and Paul's entire arm was in the tank. He had a fish in his hand, and he was making it swim back and forth in the tank. When he let the fish go, it floated to the top and was lying on its back. I believe he thought he could fix the situation by manually moving the fish back and forth.

Oh my! This was not good! These fish were Mara's, and she loved them. I asked Paul where Mara was, and he replied that she had locked herself in the bathroom. I knocked on the door, and asked Mara to please open the door so I could talk with her.

She did, and I went in and closed the door behind me. I sat on the toilet, and asked her to sit on my lap. She was sobbing, and she informed me that Paul had killed her beloved Pip. It was Pip he was trying to make come back to life, but Mara knew he was dead. I just held her, and let her cry. After some time, I told her to go upstairs while I checked on the situation.

I called my husband, and I was almost in tears because I knew how much the fish meant to Mara. I couldn't believe I had been called to care for someone with a disability. It really was a hard moment, because you realize there is nothing you can do to fix it. He has a disability, and so he does things that other children know not to do. It was not his fault.

My son Ted was home, and he kept saying, "It's just a stupid fish. Fish die all the time. What kind of a pet is a fish anyway?"

I would reply, "Its Mara's stupid fish, she loves, feeds, and talks to her fish every day. It's her special pet. She has a right to be sad." On one hand, I had kids crying, and on the other hand, *it is just a fish.*

I went to where Paul was still trying to resurrect the fish, and I said, "Paul, the fish is dead. Get a bag and put the fish in it so we can bury it." I noticed that he was crying. I told him I would go talk to Mara, but that everything was going to work out fine. We would go buy some more fish (as if Pip could be replaced).

I went upstairs and held Mara on my lap. I told her that, yes, Pip was dead. I explained to her once again that Paul has a disability, and that he didn't mean to kill her fish. I told her he was downstairs crying, and that he felt really bad, and we didn't want him to feel bad because he couldn't help it. I told her we would leave immediately, and go buy her some new fish. I asked her if she could go downstairs and give Paul a hug, and tell him she forgave him and that it was going to be okay.

It truly was a precious moment. Mara walked downstairs where Paul was standing still crying. She went over to him and gave him a hug, and told him it was okay and that she would get a new fish. He hugged her and asked her if she was going to be okay and told her how sorry he was. They both stood there crying for a while holding on to each other. It was sweet to watch.

We then piled into the van to go get new fish. Mara cried for two nights and since dad wasn't home, I let her sleep with me. She recovered a few days later. Her new fish didn't make it either, and so we opted not to buy any more—at least not until Paul moves out.

When Paul was in the eighth grade, we got a call from his teacher saying that he was really sick, and we needed to get him to a hospital right away. We rushed to the school to find him acting very lethargic. He told everyone he couldn't move his legs. My husband and a few of the teachers carried him to the truck, and my husband went directly to the hospital.

They ran a bunch of tests, finding nothing wrong. One of the doctors approached Tom, and told him they thought he was faking this sudden illness. My husband was offended that they even suggested such a thing, because he couldn't believe anyone would fake something like this.

We hadn't had him very long, and so we weren't used to some of his behaviors, and my husband always believes the best in people. I, on the other hand, think the worse. Once again, opposites marry.

Tom brought him home, where Paul insisted he couldn't walk. I did notice that it seemed to be a little difficult for him to pretend he couldn't walk. Not a great actor, a great artist though. The next day he was able to get out of bed. He walked a little, but very slowly. I took him to our primary pediatrician so he could have a look at him.

He gave him a thorough check up, and we talked about possibly taking him to a neurologist. The doctor even suggested that we admit him to a hospital and have some tests run. Thank goodness, there were no beds available when he made the call to the hospital. I have a good relationship with the kids' doctor, and he understands my kids have special needs. I told him I didn't think that was necessary, because I believed it was all for attention. We agreed to wait a few days, and see what happened.

By the next morning, he was fine and there has not been any other issues relating to this incident since.

This was our first experience with him faking a sickness. Over time, he has done it many times, but we are smarter now. Every now and then, my husband will say, "Maybe you should take him to the doctor."

I reply, "Don't say that, he will get worse." I ignore him, and he gets better almost immediately. We don't fall for his shenanigans that easily anymore. We realize it just comes with the territory.

When Paul was beginning his freshman year, he needed a sports physical. I took him to the pediatrician where he pretended he couldn't see. When the nurse left the room I said, "Paul, knock it off. You and I both know you can see. Stop acting like you can't." Well, he didn't pass the physical, and the doctor would not release him to play sports until I took him to the eye doctor.

I had lived with him a few years now, and knew the drill. I was upset because I didn't want to waste my time and money at an eye doctor, especially when I had to haul all eight kids there with me, and I knew he could see.

I told my husband who said, "Well, maybe he really can't see."

I said, "Are you kidding me? Watch this." Without Paul knowing what I was doing, I had him walk up the stairs into the kitchen, and I asked him what time it was. He was about 20 feet away from the digital clock on the stove. He looked across the entire kitchen to the clock, and gave me the proper time without squinting.

He walked back downstairs and I said, "Yeah, but he can't see the big E on the eye chart."

I took him to the eye doctor, because football was the priority. He failed his eye exam, and we bought him a pair of glasses that he didn't even need.

He came home, put his glasses in their case, and left them on his dresser to look at. He never put them on.

We were at the cabin on one of our breaks. We had a 19-inch television, so it was quite small. He was in the back of the room and when the guide for shows came up he said, "Oh look, America's funniest home videos is on."

I said, "Funny how you can see that, but you can't see a big E on the wall. When we get home, I want you to start wearing your glasses, because you are almost blind."

We got home, and he started wearing his glasses. He wore them for about a week, and then he put them on the top of his shirt while he was wrestling with one of his brothers. The glasses fell off, and got smashed to pieces. He brought them out with tears in his eyes, and he showed his crumpled up glasses to his dad.

I said, "Well, I think it will be all right since WE ALL KNOW YOU CAN SEE." Actually, I didn't say that, but I wanted to.

Time went on, and we forgot all about his failing eyesight. That is, until he was going to start his sophomore year and he needed another sport's physical. It just so happened that his appointment with the doctor was the same week my dad had been in intensive care, hanging on to life. I was physically and emotionally exhausted. I really didn't want to deal with a hypochondriac.

I remember the day very clearly. It was a Monday, and Paul's appointment was at 11:00. Football practice started at 3:00 that same day. The two of us were in the van together. I parked the van and decided to have a *come to Jesus* meeting with him before we went in.

I said, "Paul, I am really tired. I have been at the hospital for a week straight, and I am short on patience right now. I am going to make myself very clear. If you want to fake that you can't hear, can't see, have one testicle, can't walk, or whatever specific ailment you decide to come up with, go ahead. If you don't pass this physical, you will not play sports this year. I am not going to take you to another doctor. This is it. So, you decide if you want to pass or not, because you and I both know you are capable of passing this physical without any problem." He just looked at me. I could see the wheels turning in his head as he was deciding what he wanted to do. Was Mom just blowing smoke? Go ahead and try me!

We proceeded into the doctor's office. The doctor completed the physical. He turned to me and he said, "Why does he have 20/20 vision this year, but last year his eyesight was horrible?"

I just looked at the doctor and I finally replied, "Do we need to go out in the hallway so I can explain things to you?"

He kind of chuckled to himself and he said, "No, I get it."

Hallelujah! He passed his physical, and was able to play sports.

Paul and Sarah both use Band-Aids on everything. If they have a bump, scratch, or nothing at all, they get out the Band-Aids and put them on, and leave them on for days. I finally had to ban them from Band-Aids unless they were bleeding—or there was actually a cut. It was like having two, two year olds in the house playing with the princess Band-Aids, but not really needing one. They were nine and thirteen. Have I said, "You can't fix crazy," yet?

They both also over exaggerate everything. If they have a cough, they walk through the house like they are dying. They moan and groan, and have difficulty walking. I just crack up. I don't give them attention. I just say, "For heaven's sake, you have a cold. You are not dying. There is nothing wrong with your legs." If I give them any attention, it immediately makes the situation ten times worse.

Let me add, when any of the children are truly sick, they get my undivided attention. I will hold them in my arms, rock them, and make them chicken noodle soup, take them to the doctor, give out necessary medication, or stay up all night with a child throwing up. I just don't have time to play sick, because I have ten kids. I only am available when the sickness is real. Three of my other children wear eyeglasses, because they really need them.

We had never lived with a child with autism, and so this has been quite an interesting journey for us.

It can be a challenge to be around Paul for a long period of time. This may be because we didn't get him until he was thirteen, and so his disability wears on us a little more than normal, or just because it is never ending. There was a time this past summer when I was in the mountains while my husband was in Phoenix. He called me, and he sounded far away. I asked him where he was. He responded that he was at home, hiding in the garage, so he could get a break from talking to Paul. I just laughed and was glad it was him, and not me.

Let me share an example of what it is like. We will all be watching the television show, Family Feud. The question I remember being asked once was, "If you were boarding an airplane, what item would you not want to see your pilot holding in his hand?" Paul screams out, "An extra pair of eyeballs." Everyone else is saying items like *a manual on how to fly an airplane*. Every time an extra pair of eyeballs isn't mentioned he will scream out, "Oh dang. Say an extra pair of eyeballs. It's up there."

It is like that question after question until I finally say, "Hey, let's watch without guessing for a while."

Tom gave him a pair of gloves once. He wore those gloves to school, to work around the house, to eat dinner, to do his homework, and to make nonstop jokes with. I let him have his fun for a couple of weeks until I finally said, "Paul, put the gloves away. Nobody wears gloves all day long." I then explained to him when he should wear the gloves. His response was a blank stare. I upset his fun.

Even when he was eighteen and nineteen years old, he would turn on the television to SpongeBob or Funniest Home Videos, and laugh hysterically at every scene. He doesn't only laugh, he screams and falls all over the floor or couch.

It is difficult to have a normal conversation with him because he can't communicate in a way that always makes sense.

Like other children with disabilities, he has a sweet personality. He is very helpful around the house, and wants to please. He really isn't that difficult to live with, we just need a break from the craziness every once in a while. He has given us many things to laugh about when the day is done, and we are tucked away in our room for the night.

Before I move on to Sarah, I will share about their adoption.

When they came to live with us, we knew that their father was in prison and was going to remain there for many more years. We were also informed that their mother was struggling with a mental illness, and she lived on the street because she refused help.

We were told that the parental rights of the parents would soon be terminated, and the kids would be available for adoption. We knew if we didn't adopt them, they would most likely be put into separate group homes until they aged out of the system. Nobody wants a 13-year-old autistic boy. Unfortunately, that is a reality. Weekly visits with their mom were scheduled, and occasionally she would show up.

After one particular visit, Sarah and Paul were explaining to us that their mom was in a wheelchair because she had a broken foot. After her foot healed, she was going to buy a house, and then they would get to go live with her.

I didn't want to burst their bubble. I know it is every child's desire to be reunited with his or her parent. I also knew they were not going to be able to be returned to their mom. The mom was incapable of caring for the kids. We didn't say anything, except we added their mom to our prayer list, and we all prayed that her foot would heal quickly and correctly.

The next time CPS called, I asked them about their mom. I asked if she was in a wheelchair with a broken foot. I then explained that the kids were communicating with me that they were going to go home when her foot was healed.

I was shocked by what I heard next. The caseworker explained to me that at the visits, Paul spends all his time making sure his mom's wheelchair is in perfect working order, since he thinks she is incapable of walking. The mom didn't have a broken foot; she had mental illness. She apparently was going through someone's garbage can when she found a boot for her foot. She put it on, and proceeded to tell everyone she had a broken foot. She had a wheelchair that she used like homeless people use a shopping cart. It carried all her earthly possessions. She only sat in it at visits. When the kids were done visiting, she would take her boot off and walk out of the office pushing her wheel chair and gathering up her possessions to take with her.

My response was, "These kids are 9 and 13 years old. They need to be told the truth about the situation. It is not healthy for them to continue thinking that their mom is going to get well, and one day take them home." Good grief, can someone help me out here? This doesn't seem like rocket science to me, but maybe it is.

She agreed. Her next words were, "CAN YOU TELL THEM?" Talk about shocked. I thought that was her job. After I recovered, I assured her that we would sit the two of them down and have a talk with them about what was going to happen, and about their mother's mental illness.

That evening I spoke to my husband about the situation and what their caseworker had communicated to me. We decided to pray for a while that God would give us wisdom, and the words to help the two of them understand the truth of what was going to happen.

The day arrived for our little talk. I will never forget it. My husband asked Paul and Sarah to meet us in the front room so we could have some privacy. They both went in and sat on the couch. Sarah had her arms crossed, and of course, Paul had his blank stare.

My husband is an amazing man. He has a way with words, and he communicates even hard subjects with such grace and love that you almost forget how difficult the subject matter is. He did all the talking.

He began by asking the two of them if they knew what mental illness was. They both responded that they did not. So, he began to share about what mental illness is and how it affects people that have the illness. They listened intently. He then explained to them about their mother's broken foot, and told them it wasn't really broken. He informed them that they would not be able to go home with their mom, because there wasn't a home—and would never be a home to go home to. He told them how she refused to take her medication, and so they couldn't do anything to help her.

The kids then explained how they knew something was wrong, because their mom used to hear voices, and act crazy. Paul and his older brother used to run in her room and restrain her from hurting herself. Sarah told us how scared she was when she lived with her mom.

Tom then talked a little about their dad, and his prison sentence and that they would be grown adults before he got out of prison. After he explained that both of their parents were incapable of caring for them, he said that leaves us with a little problem. He looked at Sarah and he said, "What is going to happen to you? Are you just going to have to live on the street, because if that is the case where are you going to get food? I know you will get hungry and want to eat, and food doesn't just grow on the trees."

I can still see her sitting there all fat and pudgy as she responds with, "Yes, I am going to want to eat."

Tom then tells them so beautifully, how God spoke to his heart years earlier. How one day Tom said to God, "God, I want to serve you, and do whatever you ask of me."

God told Tom he wanted him to take care of children that didn't have anywhere to live.

Tom asked them, "Do you have anywhere to live?"

They responded, "No, we do not."

He told them how God came to him and said, "I have two more precious children that have nowhere to go, and they won't have anything to eat. I have blessed you with that big house that has lots of room, and you also have lots of food to eat. Can you find it in your heart to just take in two more children and give them all the love and care they will need?"

My husband responded that "Yes, he had room to love two more children, and he would be happy to be their forever family."

I was sitting on the floor by the three of them with tears running down my face. Can you picture it? They were two innocent children, sitting on the couch talking with two people—who six months earlier were complete strangers. They were being told that not only had they been ripped out of the only family they had ever known, and separated from their parents, but also from two of their siblings as well. They were never going home. They were never going home, and they may never see their biological parents again.

I can't express what it is like watching the kids hear that news, and what it is like being the ones having to deliver that news. It is heart-wrenching, and you can't help but feel such loss for them. You pray and ask God to give you the strength to be faithful with what he has asked you to do. You want to be the tool that God uses to show them His love and compassion, and guide them through life in a way that enables them to grow into emotionally, physically, and spiritually healthy adults.

A year after they came to live with us, we once again bought new outfits for two more children. We all loaded up in the van to go to the courthouse. Paul's class from school met us there, so they could witness an adoption first-hand. Sarah's classmates met us afterwards at a pizza place for lunch. Then, a few months later, our pastor came over and baptized the two of them in the backyard pool.

Let's move on to Sarah.

Sarah is our first and only child who came with what we call a *honeymoon* period. We heard about this happening, but had never experienced it firsthand. For the first few months, she was happy, easy to please, and plain old giddy. It didn't take long for that to change though, and we soon began dealing with a different child than the one who had originally shown up.

Almost immediately after Sarah moved in, I would catch her hiding in the dining room shoving whatever food she could find into her mouth.

Sarah was a different story when it came to food. I noticed that when Sarah's mom didn't show up for a visit, Sarah would sob and the words out of her mouth would be, "What are we having for snack?" I realized she was using food as a comfort.

Over time, I watched Sarah struggle with a food addiction that was out of control. One beautiful Saturday morning, we were at one of the kids' track meets. Tom and I were sitting up in the bleachers watching the festivities. When I looked down, I saw Sarah standing by the garbage can grabbing left-overs out of the garbage. I looked just in time to see her licking some leftover cheese out of a nacho cheese container. I walked down, put my arm around her, told her to put the food back in the garbage, and come sit with us. I truly was in shock. When we got home, I took her aside and talked to her about the dangers of doing that and why it was not appropriate. I don't think she got it, nor did she care. To this day, I am sure she still gets into the garbage if there is a scrap of food she can see.

I would ask her to make juice for the day, only to look up and see her eating the contents of the juice packets instead of putting them in the pitcher. I also found empty juice packets in her clothes drawer along with wrappers to pop tarts and other miscellaneous items.

When she was in junior high, she would attend the junior high Sunday school at our church. Of course, what is church without food? They almost always have a spread of goodies for the kids to partake in. When we would drop her off, we would instruct her to take only one snack. She could have one candy bar, one bagel, or one granola bar. She got to choose. When she would come out of class, I would ask her how she did. The news was never good. She would relay to me that she had eaten two pop tarts, two breakfast bars, and vanilla wafers and I am sure that is only what she was willing to tell me.

She also would come out of class with her Bible, pockets, and everything else stuffed with candy. So, when she comes out now, we check her Bible, purse and anything else for some leftover goodies. It is almost impossible for her to only eat one thing, and not to think she can sneak fifty more things home for later in the week.

Our babysitters come every Saturday night, and they know the kids well. They know what to watch for in each of them. You can't be playing outside with the kids and let Sarah in the house unsupervised—unless it's okay she is getting into the food. One Saturday Sarah asked to go in and get a drink. The babysitter noticed that she was gone a little longer than was necessary. She came in and found Sarah in the dining room pouring Parmesan cheese into her mouth as quickly as she could. The floor and table were both covered with Parmesan cheese. I think the babysitter was in shock.

She asked, "Why Parmesan cheese?"

I said, "Everything else is locked up."

Sarah would lick her plate. She refuses to leave even one crumb of anything on her plate. If she is carrying your plate over to the sink for you, and there is one grain of rice left, she would take it.

When she eats her food, she never looks up. Her face is always in her food. She doesn't bring the food to her mouth; her mouth is down in the food. She does not make conversation at the dinner table, and if you ask her to share how her day went, she gets totally annoyed. Mealtime is not a time for conversation in her mind. She becomes one with the food, and would prefer if everyone else would disappear.

I would give the kids a candy bar on a Friday night for a treat, and she would rub it all over her lips really slowly. It was like she was having sex with her candy bar. When I would say, "Sarah, you have five minutes to finish your candy or it is mine." She would get furious. It was truly like I was interrupting sex with her candy bar. Is it okay to say it was gross?

She is never finished eating. No matter what she is eating, or how much she has eaten, she always says, "Mom, am I done?"

I would reply that *yes*, she was done. She never likes my answer.

When we went to an amusement park, the older kids went to the bigger rides while we stayed with the smaller kids. They all stopped for a quick snack. The chaperone sent us a picture of Sarah with a boat filled with about five scoops of ice cream, and all the amenities that go with it. The other kids all had a two-scoop ice cream cone. She doesn't know when enough is enough, and what a healthy portion is. If she does know, she certainly doesn't care.

Another example of that is the time they were serving donuts for breakfast at school. We didn't know this, and so the kids ate before leaving for the day. All the kids got to school and helped themselves to a donut. Sarah on the other hand helped herself to four jelly filled donuts and when she told us about it saliva was running down her mouth with just the remembrance of the yumminess.

The kids all get a glass of juice with dinner. She continually drinks her drink, and then sneaks and drinks everyone else's. Everyone will turn around and their drink will be empty. It is always her. When she does that, we ground her from drinking juice for one week. It doesn't matter. When her week is up, she always repeats the behavior.

In the discipline chapter, I tell the story of her eating two lunches at school every day. She packed one and bought one until I caught her.

We have two refrigerators and one is in the front living room. It is also the place the girls practice their piano. One night, when Sarah was playing the piano, I was thinking to myself, "I wonder what she is doing. I haven't heard the piano in a while." I opened the door to the front room, and found her with both hands in the ice cream just shoving it into her mouth, as fast as she could. It was apparent to me that she was playing a song, and when the song was finished she would get up for some ice cream, play another song and so on. The piano was filthy. In the past, I had wondered why we had so little ice cream. I thought I was losing my mind, but really I was just living with the ice cream monster.

Another time, I was upstairs and the girls were all getting ready to get in the shower. I noticed as she picked up her pajamas she scooped them up like she was hiding something under them. When she was in the bathroom, I entered and she had the container of pancake syrup and she was getting ready to chug it. I looked at her, took the syrup, and walked out. There really was nothing to say. By this time, I knew there was nothing I could say that would change the situation. I could share 1000 stories regarding her problem with food, but I think you get the idea.

When she came to us, she was in the obese category for her height and weight. My desire for her was to get her into the proper weight range where she would be the healthiest. We have achieved that, but it is hard keeping her there.

I took her to the pediatrician who talked with her about health. They talked about food, but also about drugs and smoking. It was a conversation about health in general. I thought that might help, but wasn't really hopeful. It did not help.

At this time, she is assigned to a therapist to try to help her figure out the *why* of this behavior. Not only why she does it, but why she doesn't care.

We are concerned about whether the therapy will help or not, because Sarah has to want to get help, and so far she hasn't shown any interest in getting help. I sometimes feel that I am getting her help, because it is what I want for her—and not what she wants for herself. She has to see the need to get help, and have the desire to make a change. That has not happened. She would be much happier if I let her eat whatever she wants whenever she wants it. This is a source of contention between her and me.

It's no different than trying to help someone else lose weight. They have to take the initiative to lose weight on their own. There is only so much you can do to help.

Right now, I am only controlling her behavior by locking up the pantry as well as the refrigerator, giving her smaller portions, and keeping a very close eye on her. When she goes to school, I know she eats everyone else's food, and possibly still gets in the garbage for the leftovers the kids have thrown away.

If things don't change when she moves out, it will not take long for her to reach 300 pounds. She will not be obese—she will be morbidly obese.

This issue with food is a good example of what I mentioned in the chapter, *Things You Need to Know*. I talked about how hard it can be to see a harmful behavior in a child, you work like crazy to help the child change that behavior, you feel the behavior should change over time, and it just doesn't.

In the realm of foster care and adoption, you will see crazy behaviors. Don't think that you will be successful helping the child conquer all the negative behaviors they may be dealing with. You won't. It can be disappointing, and even discouraging. I can't tell you the times Tom and I have talked with her about God's healing power that is available to her. I can honestly say six years after Sarah came to live with us, she is no better today than she was then. I am exhausted just thinking about how much work we have put into this one issue with no positive results.

From the day she moved in, she made it very clear that she didn't care for Joy and Mara. She absolutely ignores them, and is nothing short of rude. They have come to her and asked her to look at a picture they have drawn, and she ignores them. I always say to her, "Answer them," and she grudgingly complies. This happens all the time where the little ones try to engage her in conversation or give her a goodnight hug, and she ignores their existence. When I am around, I always make her respond to them.

Mara and Joy can be sharing something about their day, and she just grunts at them. There is no other way to explain it, but to say she has been unbelievably rude and hateful towards them—which makes it hard.

One day, I told her that I just wanted her to be kind. I said, "I am not asking you to love them, but I am telling you that I expect you to be kind." She replied, "How can I be kind when I don't love them?"

I said, "Are you able to be kind to a total stranger?"

"Yes," she said.

"Do you love the total stranger?"

"No."

"Well, if you can be kind to a total stranger, then I am sure you can be kind to your sister."

I also gave her a word picture. I said, "What if you still lived with your biological mom, dad, and your three siblings. Your parents came to you and said that another child needed a home, and they were going to bring that child into your home. When they did, the new child was really rude and mean to you. Do you feel your parents should allow that child who was brought in to be rude and mean to you in the safety of your own home?"

"I guess not."

"I cannot allow you to continue to be mean to the other girls either. It is not right. As the parent, it is my job to make sure our home is a safe, loving, and accepting place for all children."

I was hoping that would help her get it on a different level. Whenever she is downright rude, I call her on it. If it is a situation where she needs to apologize, I ask her to do that as well. She hates it.

I have explained to her that before she moved in, we all took a vote about whether or not we should make her and her brother a part of our family, and that everyone voted *yes*, we would let them move in. The vote included Mara and Joy. We have talked about family and how we are each other's greatest cheerleader, and asked her how she would feel if we ignored her and acted like she didn't exist.

Well, six years later, she is a little better, but she would prefer if Mara and Joy would just go away. Any kindness she does show does not come easy. It is very hard for her to be nice to them and they know it. Joy is now ten, and she has started being mean to Sarah in return.

We continue to remind them that we are a family, and that loving each other is a choice that we make. I only wish they would listen!

This is one of the harder issues of Sarah's we have to deal with. Having someone in your home who is *hateful* towards other people in your home, is hard to live with. Some of the behaviors you can overlook, and you realize it just goes with the territory. This arrogance of hers is one of the more frustrating things we deal with on a daily basis. You can't lock this one up and make it go away. It is always there, showing its ugly head.

Sarah has a problem with changing her socks. I was noticing that she would wear the same pair of socks for several days in a row. One day I said, "Sarah, are those a clean pair of socks, or did you wear those yesterday?"

She responded that she had worn them the day before as well. I told her to please go get a clean pair of socks on.

She flipped out! She started crying and if looks could kill, I would have been dead. I asked her why she was so upset. I said, "Don't you have a drawer with about twenty pairs of clean socks in it?"

She said, "Yes, but this is how I have always done it."

I said, "Well, it is important that every day you change your socks and underwear, that you wear deodorant, brush your teeth and comb your hair."

She went upstairs and got a clean pair of socks on, but she cried all the way to school. It was so bad, that before school I had to go talk with her teacher and let him know that if she didn't calm down, to call me and I would make a trip back to the school to deal with the situation. This situation with the socks has happened several times, and continues happening to this day. I am constantly reminding her to change her stinky socks.

One day, a friend of mine likened it to all of us. She said, "Jill, so many of us hold on to things like not forgiving, bitterness, bad habits, old memories, and we don't want to let them go—because it is more comfortable in the known than the unknown. Just like Sarah and her socks. She didn't want to let the old, dirty socks go because it is *what she has always done*.

God looks down and says, "You silly child, don't you know there is a better way. I have something so much better for you than what you have always done. You need to trust me, and change your socks."

Just like Sarah struggled with her socks, we also struggle with our dirty things too. It is no different, and my precious friend helped me see the situation differently. To me it was just a pair of socks, to her it was so much more. I got it!

About two months ago Sarah was sharing with me that before she came to live with us she never owned a pair of flip flops, and that she feels awkward wearing them. She then told me she has always worn tennis shoes, but that she never had socks, and so she would get these horrible sores on her feet. Until one day, a teacher bought her ONE pair of socks. Makes sense now, doesn't it? There is always a reason behind the craziness. It may take time to figure out what the reason it, but there is a reason for the behavior.

When Sarah was in the fourth grade, she was fortunate once again to be attending the small private school where the teachers loved the kids and worked very closely with our children. They knew my kids were special needs, and they were so amazing at working with them.

It was a normal school day, or so I thought. I dropped the kids off at school, and later in the day, I proceeded to go get my hair cut and colored. I was relaxing with foil in my hair when my phone rang. It was Sarah's teacher. She told me that Sarah couldn't find her language paper, and she had flipped out. She couldn't get her to calm down. I asked her if she had an extra language paper she could let her have. She said, "I've tried that, and she continues to cry, and I can't console her she is so upset." I asked to speak with Sarah.

Sarah got on the phone. I said, "Sarah, what is the matter?" She was crying so hard she was hiccupping.

She replied, "I lost my language paper, and can't find it anywhere."

I said, "Didn't Miss T give you another one?"

She said, "Yes, but I can't find mine." I explained to her that she didn't need hers, and that the new paper would work just fine. I told her to go to the bathroom, wash her face, and get herself together. I prayed with her over the phone, and talked with her for a while to try to calm her down. The teacher got back on the phone and I told her that if she didn't calm down, to call me back and I would make a trip to the school.

Well, I received another call and had to make a special trip to the school. When I got there, I found the teacher sitting behind my daughter rubbing her back while my daughter was sobbing. The other kids in the class were just hanging out. My daughter had her hands folded, and she was rocking back and forth staring straight ahead. To be honest, I knew that was a comfort mechanism, but I had never seen it in person and it was quite shocking. My first thought was, "This child is crazy, and I'm not going to adopt her." My second thought was, "Don't be shocked, just go deal with it."

So, I took her out of class, and spent some time cleaning up her face, holding her, praying and talking with her. After about an hour, she was prepared to return to class. That evening we spent a lot of time talking with her about what to do when she feels anxious and fearful.

I don't know why this situation upset my daughter so much. The only thing I can figure out is that when they lived with their mom, they were kicked out of their house very quickly, and they lost everything. They didn't take any pictures, clothes, toys, books, or any other personal items with them. They then went to a shelter in the downtown Phoenix area, where the few items that they did have were stolen or almost stolen. I think that she had faced so much loss that the thought of even losing her paper was overwhelming to her, and it triggered some memories of her previous losses.

Sarah, like Paul, has a problem with stealing, and not only food. If money is lying around, she thinks it is hers for the taking. I have caught her putting money that is not hers into her purse.

I will say, "Is that money yours?"

"No."

"Then why are you putting it in your purse? That is stealing."

Just last night, I set some money on the counter. It was a small amount and I knew how much was there. There are times I just want to live like a normal family. I get tired of having to take my purse upstairs with me, lock the cabinets, and keep a close eye on her and her brother. Sure enough, I woke up this morning to find some of the money missing. When I questioned the kids, I found out Sarah took it.

I explained to her that I wasn't mad, but I was sad. I said, "I would love nothing more than to be able to trust you. Instead, from now on, if I go to bed before you older kids, you will have to go upstairs as well. Even at your age, I can't trust you to even leave you alone downstairs. It is sad to me, because there is such a better way." I told her I was sorry she made the choice to be untrustworthy.

She told me that it is a habit. I explained to her that habits can be broken. She is old enough to understand that what is mine is not hers. Don't touch things that do not belong to you. People should have boundaries that are respected. There have been several occasions where she has gone into my bathroom, looked in my drawers, and has taken whatever she has wanted. I go to get something out of the drawer, and it has mysteriously disappeared.

I reminded her that all of her needs are being met, and there is no reason to steal. There is no reason to take my stuff, or her sister's stuff, when she has her own stuff. She has a choice. Sometimes, she wants me to believe she has no choice in the matter, but I want her to take responsibility for her actions and then choose to change the behavior.

If she is in a locker room or somewhere that stuff is lying around, she will pick it up thinking it is hers for the taking. I make her take it back.

After she has been caught stealing, she has yet to apologize. She always sees herself as a victim, because there is a consequence even if the consequence is just us talking to her about respecting other people's things.

For instance, once after she stole some money from us, I went through her school backpack to see if there was more. She was furious that I had gotten into her *personal things*. My husband said, "Well you didn't mind getting into mom's personal money and taking it, or getting into the kitchen cabinets and filling up your backpack with 50 items of food. We cannot trust you, and so you gave up the privilege of having your privacy. We will look wherever, whenever we feel it is necessary." Not good. After an incident like that, she will mope around the house for up to two weeks feeling sorry for herself.

The only thing that comes to mind is once again the fact that they lost everything and they feel the need to take things just in case they need it for a later date. She and her brother are two of the sneakiest people I have ever met. They are quick.

This behavior is also more difficult to deal with, only because I feel I have to always be watching. I will turn my back, and stuff walks away. When she and her brother are in another room, I always wonder what they are really doing. So I can never really rest even in my own house.

I know this comes with the territory as well—it is just tiresome.

I kept finding ibuprofen pills under her bed. I finally asked why they were there. My daughter Cathy informed me that Sarah takes a handful of them every night. Are you kidding me? I still get shocked at some of these behaviors, and I don't know why. I should expect them. I approached Sarah, and asked her if she takes a handful of ibuprofen every night.

Her response was, "Yes."

I said, "Why?"

She said, "Because I might get a headache."

I spent some time explaining to her the dangers of that behavior, and then I told her you don't take medicine unless you need it. The medicine cabinet was then off limits to her. If she needs medicine, she now has to ask. The other day I saw her opening the medicine cabinet and looking inside.

I asked her what she needed and she replied, "Nothing."

I said, "Then close the cabinet."

Unfortunately, I realize that things are not going to change. At least not while she is living with me. This behavior will continue until the day her and her brother move out. We are not fixing the problem. We are only trying to control it. It becomes so tiring and at times, I can feel a little hopeless. This is why it is difficult in foster care and adoption to stay focused and remember it is not our job to fix. We continue to teach what is right, hoping the child will accept God's healing power in their life. We so desperately want healing for them, but we can't make it happen—only they can.

Early on, we also noticed *odd* behavior in Sarah that was similar to her brother Paul. We were not the only ones noticing the *oddness*. I have had several of her teachers mention to me that they thought something was wrong with her. Her eighth grade principal told me she thought she was on the lower end of autism. Many of our friends that have spent any time with her at all, mention that she is *different*. There are many reasons for this. I will try to explain what we have noticed.

She spends a lot of her time asking questions that she knows the answer to:

I will say, "Sarah, please go get Dad his glasses."

"Does he need his glasses so he can see?"

I will reply to my straight-A student,

"I don't know, why do you think Dad needs his glasses?"

One day up at the cabin I commented, "My, it is such a beautiful day."

She responded, "Is it a beautiful day, because the sky is blue?"

"I don't know" I said, "Why do you think it is a beautiful day?"

I will be pulling lasagna out of the oven at dinnertime. She will ask, "Are we having lasagna for dinner?"

I will ask, "Do you think we are having lasagna for dinner?"

When a meal is finished, I may say, "Sarah, Will you please clean off the table?"

She responds, "Do I need to clean off the table because it is dirty?"

You get the picture.

Most of the time, I handle these questions pretty well, but there are times I just want to scream, "STOP ASKING ME STUPID QUESTIONS!" It is the way she is, and I have to try to embrace her oddness. It isn't always easy for me.

Like her brother, she loves facts. The difference is she can carry on a semi-normal conversation with you, where as her brother has trouble. Most of her conversation consists of quoting facts, or asking fact questions, but she is capable of having a conversation.

Here are some examples: "Cindy, are you playing Mesa Prep in volleyball on Saturday?"

Sarah will comment, "Mesa Preps' colors are purple and yellow, and when we played them last time, the score was 25 to 12 for the first game, and then the second game was 25 to 20, and that occurred on September 25."

The music will be on in the car. When a new song comes on she will say, "This is Steven Curtis Chapman singing Cinderella, a story he wrote for his two younger children." This will continue with every song that comes on the radio.

She informed me one day that tomato soup has gone up about 15 cents in the past year. She knows that, because whenever we are getting groceries, all she does is pick up items, and read the label and look at the price. She knows how much sodium is in a jar of pickles, so when you get out a pickle to eat she will tell you exactly how many calories, sodium, and carbs are in that item. It is a bit crazy.

She got in the car one day after school, and she started giving me the facts for the day. She told me what math lesson and problems she did in math, what her assignment was in biology, and science. I stopped her and said, "Hey, guess what I did today? I went home and put the clothes in the laundry. Then, I started dishes. When the dishes were done, I began making dinner for tonight." I stopped and said, "Do you care what I did today?"

She replied, "No."

I said, "I send you to school, and I know you are doing math, science, and biology. I don't care what your particular assignments for today were. Why don't you tell me if anything funny or unusual happened today instead."

Those kinds of conversations don't come easy for her.

If she is not giving the facts, she is asking for facts. "Mom, whose jingle is *MMMMM good*?" We will be watching America's Got Talent, and she will ask me the ages of all the people auditioning. She never stops wanted facts.

Entertainment to her is reading a dictionary. She loves new words. She will comment that it is an *arid* day, or when she is talking about someone leaving her table at school, she will say, "They departed from me," instead of saying, "They left." She will use words I have never heard of. One time, she commented on our bunnies, but I didn't know what she was saying. I asked her what she meant, and she said, "You know, *fuzzy*."

"Then why don't you just say fuzzy?" I asked.

She responded, "Well, shouldn't I use the new words if I know what they mean?"

"Sure, go ahead." (Nobody else knows what you are saying) But I kept that thought to myself.

When we go to the library, she picks up fact books. She has a book with every Pokémon character in it. It lists their name, age, weight, what they do, etc.... I can ask her any question regarding 100 characters, and she will be able to tell me the answer to my question.

I was once singing a children's song, and she chimed in, "I played that song on the piano. Alfred's book two, volume one, it was September when I was in fourth grade and I learned it in three days."

"Oh, that's nice." What do you say to that?

When Mara was in second grade, she cut out a form of a human body. Then, she added the heart, liver, kidney, intestines, etc. to the body form. She came home and hung it in the entryway on the wall. One day we walked into the house to find the small intestine lying on the floor. Mara said, "Oh my, the small intestine needs to be taped back up," to which Sarah started rattling off facts about the small intestine: how long it was, where it was located, etc.... It never ends.

She also touches and looks at everything. One of her teachers told me she walks around the room picking up papers that the teacher has stacked around the room. She had to ask her to leave things alone that were not hers. She will go to the other student's desks and go through whatever is on them. It was such a problem, the teacher asked me to speak with her about it and get her to stop the behavior.

When the mail comes, she wants to read whom it is address to, and whom it is from. If one of the other children has left an assignment from school lying around, she picks it up, reads it, and then will give me the facts regarding what she has just read. I have had to explain about boundaries once again. Just because it is there, doesn't mean it is for *you*.

Before I go on, let me say that we have spoken to the school special needs department regarding her behavior. We were told that she does not qualify for services, because she gets straight A's. She is just very *odd,* and so it would be in our best interest to embrace her *oddness*. They told us they believe she has autism, but since she is highly functional, there is nothing they can do. I have asked more than once.

This is not a behavior that is difficult to live with. She is just *different*, or *unique*.

We began to notice that she had no empathy. We had a few difficult years where a lot of family members were dying, and our family was experiencing a tremendous amount of loss.

I remember one particular Sunday when we all stayed home from church so we could speak with the kids. We had to tell them some difficult news. We had to share that David's uncle had died, and we all knew how much David loved his uncle so we knew this was going to be difficult.

Tom took David into the front room so he could talk to him privately, and not in front of the whole family. While he was with David, sharing the news and holding him in his arms, I gathered all of the other children around me downstairs. We held hands, and as I was crying, I explained to them that David's uncle Billy had died and Dad was in the front room telling David right then. I told the kids we needed to take a few minutes, and pray for David. As we prayed, I noticed the whole family was sobbing. Everyone was feeling David's pain—the whole family, except Sarah. She continued doodling on her paper like nothing sad was going on around her.

That same day, when things calmed down we then had to explain to the children that our daughter-in-law had walked out on our son, and that she was no longer going to be a part of the family. We had waited to tell them until she filed for divorce, and we knew she wasn't coming back. We all loved and adored our daughter-in-law. She was a huge part of our family, and her leaving caught all of us off guard.

I was so angry that we had to share this news with them, because the kids had already suffered such loss in their lives. I didn't bring them into my family to experience more loss. I thought, "Great, just another person walking in and out of their life."

The response to this news from the children was like we thought it would be. It was not good. Joy screamed, and stomped up the stairs yelling how much she hated this family. There was tremendous sobbing from all of us. I just had to grab the person next to me, and just hold on. It was an incredibly difficult day for every child—except one.

Sarah hardly looked up. She didn't cry. She wasn't sad. She couldn't have cared less, and to this day, she has never even mentioned our daughter-in-law. The other children have looked at her picture, or asked if they would ever get to see her again. Their response was a typical response from someone experiencing a loss.

My parents were best friends with another couple for over forty years. The husband of this couple was out back trimming a tree when he fell dead of a heart attack. I was up in Pinetop when it happened. The day of the funeral, I called my mom to see how she was doing. She was crying, as she was telling me how she just kissed her friend's cheek and told her how sorry she was. I was crying because my mom was crying. When I got off the phone, the children asked me why I was crying, and so I shared the story with them. Sarah says, "I would never cry about something like that."

I responded, "Sarah, if Grandpa died today, do you think you would cry?"

She said, "No."

I said, "How about Aunt Mary or Uncle Paul? Would you cry if something horrible happened to them?"

She honestly looked at me like I was crazy, and she said that she didn't think so. She couldn't understand why that would be sad.

Sarah wants to work in the medical field. One day, my daughter Cathy was asking about becoming a nurse. We were talking about being a nurse in the delivery department. Cathy said, "Well, what if a baby was born dead? How would I not cry?"

I responded, "I don't know. If I was a nurse, and saw two parents holding a baby that hadn't lived, I would have a hard time not leaving the room and crying." I told her I thought it was a natural thing to want to cry when we see others' pain.

Sarah commented, "I wouldn't cry."

I said, "I know."

One day, the girls and I were in a store getting everyone a cell phone. There was a sweet older gentleman in there that struck up a conversation with us all. He began showing us pictures of his wife who had died six months earlier of cancer. They had been married for over 60 years. He was sharing about his life without her, and how hard it was for him even though he had five great kids.

As he was talking about her, he began to cry. I asked him if it would be okay if I gave him a hug to where he replied that *yes*, I could hug him. My four other girls were standing around him rubbing his arms, and showing him such compassion and kindness.

I was crying, he was crying, Cindy, Cathy, Joy, and Mara were all crying. Sarah was looking bored, and wondering when the old man would shut up and we would all stop our blubbering. I can still picture the disgusted look on her face as she was watching this show of empathy. She had no time for it.

There have been a million times in the last six years that we have noticed her lack of empathy. It is apparent on a daily basis. We believe it is because she is autistic, or because of her past, and hopefully not that she is psychotic. Believe me, sometimes we wonder.

This lack of empathy also goes with animals. When two of our rabbits died, our sons' beloved dog, and our fish died, she showed no emotion. When we gave our devil dog away, and everyone was screaming, she didn't care. She doesn't touch the pets, love on them, or even look in their direction.

One day, we were all outside and all the neighbors were looking for an older gentleman's dog that had gotten out. He was an old dog and the man was very worried about it, so everyone was pitching in to help find it.

Sarah looked at my husband and said, "Why doesn't he just put that old, dumb dog down?"

My husband responds, "Because he loves him."

Here is the funny part. I find this part of her personality also very interesting. I don't get it! Let me tell you when she does cry. She sat on her kindle, and it broke. She sobbed for three hours like one would sob if they lost their best friend. We could not console her. She was hysterical.

Another time, she told Joy that if we weren't around, she would beat her up. When we got wind of this, we told Sarah to apologize to Joy. She did, and then she threw herself on the bed crying hysterically for about four hours. When she got up, she wanted to hang on me, and cry in my arms for another four hours.

One day, Tom was having a Bible study with the kids, and he asked them the question, "Why do you need a Savior?" Then he went around the room and each child had to share a sin they had committed.

Paul mentioned the fact that he steals. Tom says, "Yes, that is a problem for you."

Cathy mentioned that the night before when we were on a date they were playing catch in the house, which is against the rules.

Once again, Tom says, "Yes, that was a no-no."

Joy shared a lie she had told.

They all took turns sharing something they had done wrong. It was quite funny, and they all were so precious sharing.

When it was Sarah's turn, she couldn't think of a sin she had ever committed. Not one in her entire life. Tom said, "Well, let me help you." He then whispered something in her ear. She went back to her position on the couch, and then she said, "I have a problem with arrogance."

Tom said, "Yes, you do."

Keep in mind here, she wasn't singled out. We were all sharing why we needed a Savior, not just her.

After the lesson, she began sobbing. She went to Tom for comfort, and he held her for a while, explained to her that nobody is perfect, we all sin, and that is why Jesus died for us. This wasn't a 15-minute ordeal. This lasted all day. She wanted to be held for hours, because she couldn't believe she had committed a sin. She truly was devastated.

We recently spoke to a counselor regarding her inability to show empathy, because it seems the older she gets, the worse it seems to be. Maybe, we just notice it more because a child her age should be able to show some level of care and concern for those around her.

He told us that there are classes where someone like her can go, which teach you when to show empathy. So, if a coworker's mom dies, they would teach her that is a time where she would want to send a card, attend a funeral, or offer a word of comfort. He said, she can learn to respond to events that require empathy, but she will never herself be able to feel empathy.

So, we are going to get more information on those classes and try to fit it into her schedule, so she can learn how to be more socially appropriate where empathy is concerned.

She also doesn't have a normal ability to bond. We noticed this early on. Once she moved in with us, she never mentioned her foster grandmother again. I would ask her if she wanted to call her or go visit her, and she would reply, "I'm sure Grandma is just fine." This was the woman she had lived with for one year, and she had communicated with us how sad she was that she had to leave her home. She stated that she was like a grandmother to her, and loved her with all her heart. Yet, she never once picked up the phone to call her. I found that odd.

I would ask her if she wanted to call her sister who was living in a group home, and once again, she would look at me with a look of wondering why I was asking her such a question. I would say, "You're in a home with a family, with your tummy full, and your needs being met. Your sister is in a group home with staff members there to do a job. It might be nice if your sister heard from a family member or someone that cares about how she is doing." I got no response from her, and no phone calls were ever made.

It was teacher appreciation week at school. My daughter, Cindy, was making a poster for her teacher. She was writing things on the poster that said, "Thanks for helping me with my math. I will miss you next year when I leave. You are the greatest teacher with the best jokes."

Sarah made an individual card for all of her teachers, because she was old-er and went from class to class. All of her cards read, "I love you like a mom; I love you like a dad. You are everything to me. What will I do when I don't see you every day?" There was absolutely no mention of what a great teacher they were, or how much she enjoyed being in their class. Once again, I realized that she didn't understand relationships, and how they work.

In her mind, she is totally bonded with these teachers, even though once she left school she will never talk, contact, or think about them again. In her mind, she loved her foster grandma to death, even though she never again contacted her or asked to see her. In her mind, she loves her sister even though in the six years she has lived with us, she has not called her once. In her mind, she is bonded with us even though, as you will read, she will only come to our funeral. She doesn't get it.

She is now 15 years old, and I can honestly say that her phone has never rung unless it was one of us calling her. Like her brother, she thinks she has many friends, yet she has never been invited to go anywhere with anyone she knows. I believe she wants friends; she is socially awkward, and doesn't know how to go about any type of real relationship.

She used to hang out with all the teachers. At recess during school, she would talk to the teacher on recess duty. She would talk with the librarian, and in her mind, they were great friends. She believed and communicated to me that she and adults have a lot in common, and those are her friends.

I replied, "No, you don't have a lot in common with adults. You just think you do. These teachers think you are a very nice little girl. They talk to you, because that is the polite thing to do. If you were to ask them who their friends are, they will not name you. They will never invite you to a movie or the mall on a Saturday night."

I encouraged her to spend more time looking for children her age to hang out with. She replied that she has nothing in common with kids her age. She wants to talk about authors, and facts, and nobody is interested in her facts. I said, "Well, you probably aren't going to find someone that wants to discuss the facts of the solar system, but, friendship goes two ways. You listen to your friend and their interests, because you love them and care about them, so what they have to say becomes important to you. They love you, and so they listen to the things you have to say that are important to you." I explained that I have friends that talk about things that I am not particularly interested in, but because I love them, I listen, care, and respond.

She is unable to comprehend that concept. She cannot reciprocate kindness. She feels she deserves kindness, but she has none to give in return. What we have witnessed in her is that she is only able to think of herself. She has no desire to listen to what is important to another soul. Her best friend is herself, and she can't understand why everyone doesn't want to be around her, and listen to the things she has to say. Friendship to her is someone listening only to her. She is going to go through life very alone. She will be fine as long as she has herself tagging along. It is quite sad, yet there is nothing we can do.

We continue to talk to her about friendship, relationships and encourage her to reach out to others. We make it a point to put her into situations where she has to think about another person. We will be getting ready to cross a street, and I will ask her to hold her little sister's hand. If someone needs a drink poured, I will ask her to get up and do it for them.

We have always said that she is one of the children that when she moves out, we will never hear from her again unless we contact her—which of course we will do. One day, my husband was mentioning to the kids that Ted was going to be moving out in a few months, and telling them that they needed to be prepared for that. Then, he stated that Paul would be moving out this summer. Paul is Sarah's biological brother. Tom asked her if when he moves out if she thinks she will call Paul to see how he is doing. She got that odd look on her face, and responded that, "No, she couldn't see herself calling him."

My husband responded, "Well, I am sure you will call me when you move out. You will want a relationship with me."

Her response to this day cracks me up. She thought for a moment, and then with a smile on her face, thinking that she was about ready to give us a huge compliment she says, "Well, I know one thing for sure, I will go to your funeral, and I might even shed a tear." We must have had a strange look on our faces, because she asked us if there was something wrong with what she said.

I said, "No, I am so happy to hear that you will be attending our funeral. It will be so nice to see you there."

On our anniversary, Cindy, Cathy, Mara, and Joy all made us a huge anniversary card. In addition, they made us cards of their own. When we went to bed, there were notes by each side of the bed that said, "Do not get out of bed." The next page stated that since it was our "special day, the day we committed ourselves to one another," the girls wanted to make us breakfast in bed. A menu was attached for us to choose from.

So, the next morning the four girls got up and made us breakfast while we waited, for a very long time, in bed. It was so sweet and thoughtful of them.

This is a situation that Sarah would never participate in. Whether it is something being done that is special for Tom and I, a friend, or someone we don't even know—she would never think about or participate in an act of kindness without being made to.

We do understand that is how she is, but it makes it hard, especially for me. My husband can detach himself easier than I can. Sometimes, I feel like I have wasted my time even though deep down I know that is not the case. This child, if nothing else, is safe. She is getting to enjoy a happy childhood, and she will continue to be taught and loved and given many opportunities to succeed. The emotional aspect of the relationship is not there. It will never be there.

I remind myself of why she is in my home. She is here because God wanted her here. That means it is not a mistake. That means that God will give me the strength on a daily basis to live with a child that feels nothing for us. We are in essence, housing her. Every child deserves to have a family, and be loved by that family no matter what their issues are. Every child is valuable. Every child is precious and perfectly made by the hand of God.

I am reminded of some verses in the Bible that state: if you love those that love you, what credit is that to you? If you do good to those who do good to you, what credit is that to you? If you lend to those from whom you expect repayment, what credit is that to you? If I can love and lend without expecting anything in return, then my reward will be great. Luke 6:32-35 [NIV] I am to be kind to the ungrateful and show mercy.

I wrote about bonding in another chapter, and why it may be difficult bonding with certain children that you bring into your home. This is a good example. Paul and Sarah came to live with us for no other reason than for God calling us to be their parents. We acted out of obedience, and not out of a tremendous love for these children.

The two of them are incapable of bonding with us. Paul is incapable because of his disability. Sarah is also incapable, but I am not sure why. Like I have explained, she just doesn't understand relationships, and really doesn't understand what love looks like.

It is interesting to me that Paul and Sarah are siblings. They both have the inability to bond, they both feel the need to steal, and they both have trouble with relationships. Their issues are very similar. Some of that is because of autism, some is because of nature and what they experienced before they came to live with us.

Have we grown to love and care about them? Yes. We will always take care of them, and include them totally in our lives. But, we feel more like life-coaches with them than like parents who will have a lifelong parent/child bond. We know it is not like that for them or for us. There is nothing wrong with that; it is the way it is. We do the best that we can with the circumstances we have been given.

I realize this is a lot of information, and some of it can seem overwhelming and almost negative. It really isn't. It is just our life, and you learn to live, laugh, and cry through it. There are also many rewarding moments in what we see and do.

I want you to know you are not alone. I want to give the information so that you realize you are not alone, and to possibly get some ideas for what has worked or what hasn't worked for us. It is again good to be reminded that it is not our job to fix. We are not the only ones who have worked, and will continue to work hard, but do not see a positive result. We may never see results. God says, "Never tire of doing what is right." 2 Thessalonians 3:13 [NIV] There are certain things we cannot change, but need to accept, and not let it discourage us. That is why I write about having a strong support system.

In conclusion, these two children are harder to live with, but not impossible to live with. We have to stay focused and pray on a daily basis. I have to remind myself that they are wonderfully made, and I need to embrace their *oddness*. We have to remind ourselves it is not our job to fix or change them, so they better fit into our mold. These children are precious, we were called—and once again, nothing we do is wasted.

Paul at age thirteen and Sarah at age nine

Paul and Sarah ages nineteen and fifteen

Consider the cost

I believe we live in a very selfish world. Let's face it. There are many people who don't want to be bothered by the problems of others. They are self-absorbed. They get up, go to work, come home, watch TV, maybe read a book, and go to bed. Cars pull into their garage and the garage door goes down. You don't know half your neighbors. People don't even take the time to wave anymore.

We can all be selfish at different times, and Tom and I are no exception. There have been times when the cost of bringing these kids in has been great, and I have asked myself if it is really worth it. These thoughts are from our perspective as two people who could be empty nesters, but instead have eight children running around their house. Let me share some of those times and the conclusion that I have come to today.

When Tom and I were first talking about bringing the kids in, we were both climbing a mountain here in Phoenix five to six times a week. We were in great shape. We told ourselves when we got the kids we would put them in backpacks and climb with them. That never happened, and we slowly got out of shape. That can be frustrating, because we worked so hard to get in shape to begin with.

I was taking piano lessons when the first two kids came in. They were so needy and they hung on me constantly to where I was unable to practice. I had to give up lessons. It is eleven years later, and I am beginning piano lessons once again.

We were teaching Sunday school at church, and had been doing so for years. We loved the kids, and spending that time with them. We had to take about a year off because we didn't have time during the week to prepare. The girls took all our time and energy. With each additional child, we would again have to take breaks from teaching.

I drive around in a 12-passenger van, sweating to death. I really wish I could drive a smaller car that gets great gas mileage, but where, oh where, would I put those kids?

My husband and I have to struggle to find time to get away alone. It is difficult finding a sitter—who is available, plus a sitter who understands the special needs these kids have, and who watches them appropriately.

I was training for a licensing agency in the Phoenix area. It was a ten-week commitment, or 30 hours of training. That meant that I had to be away from the house one night a week. It became too much for my husband to keep up with all the children and their homework without me to help. It really is a two-man job. I had to give up training, something that I enjoyed doing.

For our twenty-fifth wedding anniversary, we planned a trip to Hawaii. It just so happened that our precious daughter with asthma wasn't doing well, and we had to cancel our trip. We were fortunate enough that we had purchased insurance, and so we didn't lose all our money. Instead, when she was better, we took a weekend cruise.

Instead of visiting Europe in the summer, we are visiting Lego Land. That makes me laugh.

Our house is always cluttered, no matter how much we pick up. The upstairs bathroom is still missing a towel rack. Someone hangs on it; it falls, leaving a hole in the wall. My husband repairs the wall, only to have the same thing happen a few months later. The plaster on the corner of the walls is coming off once again. We have even put plastic strips up to help. It doesn't help. There is constant wear and tear on the house, because so many people are living here. At this point, my husband doesn't want to repair anything. He says, "When they move out, we will hire someone to come in and fix everything all at once." I just laugh.

As I have mentioned, we own a cabin in the mountains. We would love to live there six months out of the year. We almost did, but the kids did not want to leave their schools, friends, or church, and so we decided to wait until they grow up to move. It is hard for the two of us, because we are so ready to get out of the heat for more than a few months in the summer.

You will have less free time in your day. You will have doctors, dentists, and therapy appointments. You will probably be asked to drive them to their visits with their biological family. You will need to participate in the foster care review board, as well as have monthly visits with your licensing worker, as well as the child's CPS caseworker. You will need to maintain your license by continuing your training. You will have meetings with their teachers—the kids no doubt will not be on target academically, and so you will spend a lot of time tutoring them so they can catch up. A lot of time is spent re-teaching them social and hygiene skills. The list is quite long.

Those are some examples of some silly things we have had to give up. Now let's touch on some more difficult issues we have had to deal with before sharing my conclusion with you.

My husband's father got very ill and was transferred to hospice. He was there for a while before moving back into his home until it was his time to pass away. It wasn't long before we knew he was going to pass soon. The family had all gathered on this particular Wednesday, to be by his side, and to all be together.

I was there all day with my husband and his family, but had to leave once the kids got out of school. I called everyone I knew to see if someone could watch the kids after school so I could be with Tom. My friend, Erin, said she could come over once they were out of school, and stay until 5:00. So, I once again went to my father-in-law's house to be with my husband and our two boys. At 5:00 I returned home to care for the kids. At 8:00 that night, my husband called to tell me that Dad had passed away. I asked him who was there. He said, "Everyone, but you." He didn't mean that in a bad way, he was just telling me who was there. I talked to him a while, and we continued to check in with each other until he was able to come home.

It was a really difficult time for me. I was upset that I wasn't with my husband when his father passed away, and that is where I felt I should have been. I began to resent the fact that I had all these kids. I realized that our parents weren't getting any younger, and how bringing the kids in may affect us when it comes time to care for our parents.

One year later, my husband's brother dropped dead of a heart attack at the age of 54. When it came time for my husband to drive to New Mexico for the funeral of his brother, I wanted to go to support him once again. Believe it or not, I couldn't find someone to watch the kids from about 5:00 A.M. until 10:00 P.M. So, my husband left without me.

When my husband was viewing his brother's body, he called me and was quite shaken. He said, "I wish you were here with me." Once again, I felt like the sacrifice was great.

My older sister lived in North Carolina. On a beautiful day in March, we received a call that she was in the hospital. They told us she had a stroke at the age of 49. Over the next couple of days, the story changed. We were then informed that the doctors found cancer. I spoke to her by phone every day. Within a week of her being admitted to the hospital, we were told the cancer was in her breasts, bones, brain, spine, and probably everywhere else. My brother from Florida got on his motorcycle to go visit her. I was looking for a sitter so we could fly there as soon as possible. While looking, she passed away. It was so unbelievably fast and it caught me off guard. In hindsight, I should have just left. Instead, I felt like I needed to get someone into the house to watch the kids for me. It was the wrong choice, and one that to this day I am sorry for. In the back of my mind, I was thinking if I didn't have the kids I would not have hesitated to go, and I would have been able to be there for her last breath. She died at the age of 49, and I miss her.

We have a cabin in the mountains, and spend our summers there. We were one week away from returning home to Phoenix to begin another school year. My parents were coming up to our cabin to visit with us for a few days before we left, and then they were going to enjoy our cabin for a few weeks without us.

The evening they arrived, my mom told my dad to get up and take his medicine, which consisted of two drops of medication in 8 oz. of water. My father got up and thought the actual jar of medicine was the water, and took two big gulps. Within minutes, he was vomiting. We called poison control, which told us to get him to the hospital immediately.

I remember half walking, half carrying my dad to the car. We walked by the kids who were all sitting in the living room. It was a precious sight. They all had their heads bowed as they were praying for Grandpa.

To make a long story short, he was airlifted out of Pinetop, down to Phoenix's intensive care burn unit. I left with my mother at midnight, and when we arrived in Phoenix early the next morning, my dad was on life support. They informed us that he was very sick, and they weren't sure if he was going to make it through. He was in intensive care for over a week, and almost lost his life on more than one occasion.

It was really hard on my husband. He wanted to come down to Phoenix with Mom and me, but knew he couldn't, since he had the kids to take care of. The next morning he loaded the kids and our stuff up and came home. All morning he and I were communicating on the phone regarding Dad's condition, and the severity of the situation. He wanted so desperately to be there with Mom and me. He loves my dad like his own dad, and so he felt an urgency to be there. When he finally made it to Phoenix, he had to find sitters—which was rather difficult. Usually, either he or I was at the hospital, and the other one was at home caring for the children. We didn't get to go together. It was a very difficult time for both of us.

We would love to function like a normal family. There have been times during the last eleven years where we have let our guard down. In other words, I have left money lying around—thinking that by now my children won't take it, only to find out the next day that some is missing. I have left the garage door unlocked, only to find out a child has snuck out once again.

My husband and I just recently went away for two days to celebrate our thirty-first anniversary. Upon our return, we found out that someone took $60.00 out of our son Ted's pants pocket. We figured it was one of three children. The first one I questioned was Sarah. I asked her to meet me in her room with her backpack. I asked her if she took any money that didn't belong to her. She responded that she had not. I began to look through her backpack, which made her very uncomfortable. When I opened it, I found about 20 items of food she had taken and hidden in her backpack. When we asked her if that was all she had that didn't belong to her, we also found out that she took more money out of my stash in the van. Yes, she did steal, but not the $60.00—that would be another thief in the house.

We never had to deal with issues like this with our two biological sons. It makes us feel extremely disrespected.

These times have reminded me that nothing about what we do is *normal*. We can't turn alarms off, our home is locked up like Fort Knox, and we can't *live like a normal family,* because we are not. That realization at times can be difficult. This has cost us normalcy.

These are just of few of the things that have come to mind concerning the *cost* of bringing the kids into our family. Your cost will be different from my cost. But, there will be things you will have to give up or change, even if for just for a season.

It is not uncommon for children to be thought of as a burden. They cost a lot of money and time. They "tie us down" in a lot of ways, taking away our freedom. However, the Bible states that children are not a burden, but a blessing from God. Children are a *heritage and a reward.* Psalm 127: 3 [NIV] They are not something we earn or deserve. They are a gift that God gives to us. They belong to God, and He graciously gives them to us. This is different from what many people think about children today. Our children are not a burden. They are a blessing given to us by God. I should never forget this.

Do I think of my children as a gift from God? Do I value them as special blessings from the Lord? If so, then I should thank God for the children He has graciously given to me! I should spend time every day thanking God for them, and that in turn, will have an effect on the way I view them. Over time, I will no longer see them as a hindrance to getting what I want in life (smaller vehicle, being in shape, free time, etc.) but I will recognize them as gracious gifts from an Almighty God. And this will change all that I do in relationship with my kids.

Is there a cost? Yes, there is. Is the cost worth it? Yes, it is. I do not belong to myself, but have been bought with a price. My life here on earth is short, and when it is complete, I hope I have left a legacy that reflects Jesus Christ. I do not want to live for the pleasures of this world. There is more beyond what we see here and now.

David

I mentioned in one of the other chapters how you need to realize what your limit is. It would be great if we all had the ability to adopt 100 children who need homes, but that is not realistic. I have a friend who her and her husband have adopted twenty non-adoptable kids. I do not know how they do it, and her stories make mine look lame, and like I haven't done anything at all in taking in my eight kids.

I don't know if I even remember how we heard about David and two of his siblings, but hear we did. I remember talking about them with Tom and the question was, "Can we do more?" We weren't sure. We were really busy with the seven we had already adopted, and we still had our two biological sons. Even though they had grown up, they still needed us and we wanted to continue to have a healthy relationship with them.

We spoke with our licensing worker who also didn't know if we could do more. He knew that the kids we had previously taken in were doing well, but *more*?

We all decided that we would meet the kids, and go from there. David was eleven at the time, and he had a two-year-old sister, and a five-year-old brother. They were looking to be placed together. That would take us from nine children, to twelve.

David was living with his grandparents, but his two siblings had been in another foster home for the previous two years. We were given little information regarding David. Because the two siblings were in a foster home, we got more information on them. The five-year-old brother had been severely abused, and he had a lot of acting out issues. The two-year-old sister came into care when she was two months old. She had a broken femur when she was taken away. Two other siblings, twin girls, were in-between the two we were looking to take in. The twins were in another foster/adoptive home.

We agreed to meet with the current foster family, our licensing worker, and their CPS caseworker. That was the first step. We talked a lot about the issues the five-year-old boy had. We were torn. We didn't know if we had what it would take to deal with him, and continue to be available parents to the other children in the home.

Once we did that, we were asked to meet the kids, which we did. When we met David, my husband's heart went out to him. Here was an eleven year old boy, about 5' 4", and 250 pounds. He really wanted a family. He had met a few foster/adoptive parents who had communicated that they wanted to take him into their home, only to back out shortly after.

We left the visit in turmoil. Man, we wanted to help these kids. We just didn't know if we could do it. So, at the next meeting we all decided we would take them in, and just see how it went. We couldn't promise anything.

All the other kids were okay with bringing in more children, but I don't think they understood what three more children would do to the family. We didn't really understand it at that time either.

It was October when Tom and I loaded up to go get the two smaller children from their current foster family, and bring them into our home. David was making weekend visits for a month, and then he would also be moving in.

Before David moved in, we talked to him about his weight. We told him that we were not going to put him on a diet, but that he would not be given any Dr Pepper. We found out that was his favorite drink. We also told him that we would monitor the food he ate, and that he would be expected to participate in activities with the other kids.

David agreed, and so he moved in. He was just like the other children who came with almost nothing. I remember calling his grandma, asking if he had socks and underwear. She informed me that, "No, he needed those items." I think we spent $400.00 on him the first day he came, just getting him decent clothes and individual items that he would need.

Shortly after he moved in, we took him to the dentist. I don't think he had been to the dentist more than a couple of times in his life. He had eleven cavities. They had to do a deep-cleaning, which took four visits. They had to numb his mouth, and clean his teeth in four sections.

I originally took him to a dentist on his insurance. On one of the visits, the dentist looked at David and very rudely said, "If you don't lose weight, you are going to die of heart disease at a very young age." He continued, "If you don't start taking care of your teeth, they will fall out by the time you are 25. You need to start being more responsible." David got tears in his eyes, but didn't say anything.

I was annoyed. How is this child supposed to get to the dentist, if nobody takes him? I noticed when meeting his family that nobody in his family had any teeth. I don't think dental hygiene was on the top of their list of things to do on a regular basis. If everyone in his life lets him eat himself sick, whose fault is that? I had a little talk with the dentist about his rudeness, and we never returned. We found another dentist who was more understanding to the needs of foster children. We paid for the visits ourselves, but it was worth it.

David also had other hygiene issues. I couldn't get him to use deodorant. He stunk on a daily basis. I finally told him that every day he failed to put deodorant on and I smelled him, I was going to charge him $2.00. He quickly learned how to spray a can of deodorant. It was the same with what he wore. He liked looking like a slob. I would make him dress more appropriately. That was really hard for him. He would say, "What is wrong with what I am wearing?"

I would reply, "Have you looked in the mirror? Just because you are heavy, doesn't mean you can't look nice."

When a foster child first enters your home, you are required to take him to a doctor for an initial examination. I took him to our pediatrician. The doctor was checking him out, and one of the questions he asked was, "Have you ever broken any bones?"

David replied, "Yes, I fell off my bike once, and broke my wrist."

The doctor asked him, "Why are you in foster care?"

I was sitting there, and remember I hadn't gotten much information on David. I was trying not to look too curious, but I was anxious to hear what he had to say.

What he talked about next made me cry, and the doctor's eyes also welled up with tears.

He told how his mother lived with her boyfriend. They drank and did drugs. Together, they had four additional children. The boyfriend burned the kids, broke femurs and arms, and one sister had a skull fracture when taken away at two months. The boyfriend would put a sock or rag in David's mouth while he punched him in the stomach. That way, nobody could hear him scream out in pain. He was locked in a closet with a bucket to pee in. He would be left in there for hours.

Some of the things you hear them say can be hard to imagine really happening, yet you know unfortunately, it does. One morning, we woke up and David said he got up to go to the bathroom in the middle of the night, and there was a small cockroach in the bathroom. He decided to wake up Paul to kill it for him. I said, "You shouldn't wake up Paul, you are 13 years old, just kill it."

He responded, "When I was with my mom, we lived in a house with lots of roaches. When my mom's boyfriend would get mad at me, he would come into my room while I was sleeping, and he would dump a bucket full of roaches on my head. I don't like roaches, they scare me."

I replied, "Wake up Paul." Talk about tears. Does this stuff really happen? Unfortunately, it does. It makes me sick, and so very sad.

From the moment the three of these kids came to live with us, we realized that David was in the role of parent. He was constantly instructing, disciplining, and watching over the smaller children.

I would say to him, "David, I know someday you are going to be an amazing dad. But, right now, I just want you to be the kid. We will take care of the children, and if we need your help, we will ask."

It took him quite a while to stop parenting, and feeling responsible for everyone.

He cried all the time. If I asked him to get his feet off the couch, he would start crying. To this day, he has a very sensitive spirit, and we have to be careful what and how we say things to him. In the beginning, I would say, "David, I am going to tell you something, but you don't need to cry. It is okay. I need you to pick up your dirty laundry off the floor, and put it in the laundry room." If I didn't preface it, there would be tears.

We started him out at the private school with the other children. He would come home from school and I would say, "Get out a pencil and a piece of paper. It is time to go over your spelling words."

He would say, "I don't study spelling words. I have never studied spelling words."

I replied, "Well, now you do."

He would begin to bang his head against the wall. I would say, "When you are finished banging your head against the wall, get a pencil and a piece of paper so we can get your spelling completed." Then I would wait.

Eventually, he would stop banging his head, and we would go over his words. We hired him a personal tutor to help him catch up in math.

He didn't believe in putting punctuation at the end of a sentence. He couldn't write or read cursive. I once asked his teacher what his memory work was for the next day. His teacher, feeling sorry for him, said, "Oh, I don't make him do it." I replied, "Do all of the other children in the class do memory work?"

"Yes," he said.

"Then, my son will do it too." I have never believed in enabling them to be less then all they can be.

He caught up pretty quickly. He realized early on that we took our role as parents very seriously. We knew his teachers, talked to his teachers, worked with him, and expected him to do his best.

The first couple of months we had him, he called us several times from school telling us he had thrown up in the bathroom, and he needed to come home. On the third call, I told his teacher that I believed he was faking it, and I wanted to leave him there and see what happened. She told him he could not come home, but would instead have to finish out the school day. It was the last time he called and told me he was throwing up and needed to come home.

This is one kid who really loved and appreciated being parented. Even though I know it was very difficult for him, he always responded positively to our instruction and our involvement. He has always seen it as someone caring and loving him, and he has been thankful even when it was hard.

When he came in, we didn't put him on a diet, but he had balanced meals. We took him off all soda. Because he went to a small school, he was able to participate in all sports. He went out for softball, soccer, basketball, track, and cross-country. The weight fell off. He was down almost 100 pounds after only ten months.

About a year after David moved in, I was attending the kids' cross-country meet. Paul was in great shape, and he was running in the competition as well as David. Paul went screaming by and ended up in the top five. I can remember standing there, watching David come around the final corner, running for all he was worth. Tears flooded down my cheeks as I watched this child—who eight months earlier couldn't even run—run, and he came in something like forty-second place. I couldn't have been prouder of this boy! In my mind, he won big time that day.

One day he was walking out of his room and I said, "David, I know it hasn't been easy since coming to live with us. We have taken away all the soda and unhealthy foods that you were used to eating. I want you to know that I am so proud of you. Not once have I heard you complain, and I know it hasn't been easy."

He just cried. I don't think he had ever been encouraged, or even had kind things said to him.

He has been a very easy child to bond with and love. The relationship between Tom, David, and I is truly one of a parent/child. He sees us as his parents, and is thankful we took him in. He realizes what he has been given. When he acts inappropriately with us, he is always quick to apologize.

I will get to what happened with his brother and sister in a moment, but first let me tell you about adoption day.

My husband and I got up and were getting ready to adopt yet another child. I said to Tom, "So, how do you feel? Feel any different?"

He responded, "Not really, just another child. Let's go and adopt him." We had done this so many times before.

We headed to the courthouse, and were met there by a few friends and family members. We were going through the motions that we had done so many times before. The judge asked us the typical questions, and then he looked towards David and said something like, "As of right now your name will be David Norton."

We all stood up to get ready for pictures, and when we turned to look at David, he was sobbing. My husband walked over, grabbed him, and held him in his arms. To us, it was just *another kid*, but to David, it was a *FAMILY*—something he had wanted for years.

Oh, how stupid I felt. What a precious moment it was for David, and a day that he would never forget. He wasn't just another kid—he was *our kid,* and a precious one at that.

Let's get back to his siblings. David's two-year-old sister had been in foster care since she was two months old. She was normal, and a joy to have around. It was a lot of additional work for me having another small one in the house. On two separate occasions, we left her in the car, thinking one of the other children had gotten her out.

The five-year-old brother was very difficult. He had so many behavioral issues and he reminded me a lot of Mike. He would throw fits constantly, pull out his dresser drawers, and throw all his clothes on the floor. He was constant work, and we realized early on that we could not meet his needs. He needed a smaller family who had more time to invest in him.

After they had lived with us for six months, we approached CPS and told them we would not be willing to adopt the two little ones. If they wanted to keep the three siblings together we would understand, but we were only willing to adopt David. They said they would ask David what he wanted to do.

We sat down with David, and explained to him that we were not willing to adopt his two younger siblings, but that if he wanted to stay we would be willing to adopt him. Of course, he cried. He understood that we had too many children, and didn't have the time to invest in them. He told CPS he wanted to stay with us, and keep contact with his siblings once they found an adoptive family.

CPS pulled files from prospective adoptive families who were willing to adopt two children, ages two and five and they narrowed it down to three families. They asked me to be a part of the meeting where they decided which family would be picked to take these children into their home. It is called a red file staffing.

I agreed, and really had no idea what I was agreeing to. I didn't particularly have strong attachments to these kids, and I wanted them to find another forever family. I didn't realize how difficult this meeting would end up being for me.

The three potential families, CPS, the caseworkers, and I were in this meeting. We discussed the strengths of each of the families picked. During the meeting, it became extremely emotional for me. I realized that I was helping to make a decision that would affect these two children for the rest of their lives. I knew that if they stayed with us, they would be raised in a Christian home, and they would be safe. It was more difficult than I could have ever imagined.

Finally, a family was picked, and they agreed to adopt the children. It ends up they only live two miles from us, and David sees his siblings on a regular basis. The family had wanted children of their own for 15 years, and they were more than happy to take these two children in, love them, and give them everything they would need to grow into healthy adults. These two kids are flourishing under their care. After five years, we can look back and see that we did the right thing. We never could have given them all they deserved.

We realize that a disruption is never a good thing. Making the decision to disrupt the placement of these two kids was heart-wrenching. We knew the more moves a child has, the more difficult it is for them. With that being said, we also knew that we just had too many kids, and keeping them would have been selfish on our part. We trusted that God would go with them, protect and watch over them, and He has.

Above: David age eleven, hundred pounds over weight

Below: David age sixteen and healthy

Discipline

There are many ways to discipline children. We are not all going to agree on how to handle specific situations. What works for one child, may not work for another. Discipline is huge. You want it to be different from punishment. Even the word punishment seems so condemning. We want discipline to teach a lesson and hopefully, change behavior. I am going to share with you what has worked for us, and what hasn't.

We never threaten consequences and then don't follow through. I think this is one of the biggest mistakes parents make. If I tell a child—if they do their chores all week without being told, then they can pick the movie Friday night for family movie night—then I better have movie night, and allow them to pick the movie.

If I tell them we are not going to the store until they clean their room, I better not go to the store until their room is clean. Kids are smart, and they know how to take a mile if you give them an inch. Be consistent. Don't say it, if you don't mean it!

Let me first say that I don't baby my kids. I didn't baby my biological boys. I didn't baby the new kids when they were foster kids, and I won't baby them now that they are mine. We all have to work hard to get anywhere in life. I don't want my kids looking for a hand out. One of the best ways we have found to discipline the older children is natural consequences, and taking away privileges. Let me give you some examples.

David stayed with his aunt one summer. We gave him $200.00 dollars in an envelope, and told him to give the envelope to his aunt. We also told his aunt to take the envelope from him and to give him $20.00 a week out of it for spending money. We told him many times to only spend $20.00 a week. The first mistake was that he didn't give the money to his aunt, and his aunt didn't ask for it.

After he was with his aunt for five weeks, we picked him up for our family vacation to San Diego. He should have had $100.00 left.

I asked him if he still had his money, and he replied that he did not. He had spent it all.

I asked him why he did that when I made it clear that he was to take $20 dollars a week so that it would last all summer.

He said he had gotten thirsty, and needed drinks and food when he was out at football practice. I said, "Well, you could have taken a water bottle and packed a snack if $5.00 a day wasn't enough for you." He only practiced Monday through Thursday in the mornings.

I told him that was quite the bummer, because we were all going to San Diego and he didn't have any spending money. It was very difficult, but we didn't give him any more money. The other children bought ice cream cones and played in the game room at the facility we were staying at, and he couldn't participate in those activities (there were many other things for him to do though). I told him there was a lesson to be learned. I explained that we all have a budget we have to follow. If we chose to spend money that was for food on something else, then we don't have money to eat. He had to learn to budget his money so he doesn't run out. Hard lesson, but hopefully a lesson learned.

When David was in seventh grade, he decided to go in the kitchen of the school and take some chocolate milk for his friends. He was caught, and he had to pay back the school $15.00 out of his allowance.

Another financial lesson, hopefully learned, was that same summer. We were again going to San Diego. I gave Paul $100.00 dollars. I told him $50.00 was for vacation, and he needed to put the other $50.00 away for the week after vacation, because it was for his food. He was 19 years old, and had a job, so while we lived in the mountains for the summer, he stayed in the house in Phoenix with our son Ted supervising him, so he could continue working. He needed money to buy food for himself, because we were gone.

While on vacation, I noticed he was in the game room a lot. I said, "Paul, you're not spending more than $50.00 dollars are you?"

He replied that he was not. I reminded him a couple of times that he could only spend $50.00. He said he knew that, and he assured me that he still had his money for food.

The day after we got home Paul knew we were getting ready to go back up to the mountains for the remainder of the summer. He went to his dad and told him he was out of money.

Tom yelled up at me, "Hey Jill, Paul says he's out of money."

I said, "Paul, did you spend all $100.00 dollars?"

He said, "Yes."

I replied, "Well, it stinks to be you. Now you don't have money for food, and I'm not giving you anymore." I went to the cupboard and saw that there was a big bag of pancake mix left. I informed him that he would have to eat pancakes or waffles all week until we gave him money for the next week's groceries.

The next morning, I woke up and I still laugh at the sight of him. He had the waffle maker out, and he was making a sky-high stack of waffles. The little kids walked in the kitchen and asked him what he was doing. He showed them the waffles that were for breakfast, the waffles that were for lunch, and the waffles that were for dinner. It was so cute.

I said to him, "Here is the lesson, Paul. When you move out, and I give you your money for rent, and you decide to spend it on something else, you will show up at my door asking for more, and I will say, I'm sorry you chose to spend your rent money." I will not give you more. Learn the lesson now, so it is not so painful later.

One of our children, that I will not name, was staying up late at night ordering pay-per-view porn. We didn't even realize we had pay-per-view, so when we got the $500.00 bill (that was the limit for pay-per-view) we were shocked. My husband called the cable company, and found out it was porn. Talk about getting caught with your pants down. To make a long story short, we found out which kid it was, and he lost his privilege of staying up late—as well as he had to pay us back the $500.00 when he got his first job. We also learned a lot from this lesson!

Sarah has an eating disorder. Our food is all locked up. I was packing her lunch for school every day. She also had a lunch account at school, so she could purchase lunch on the days we didn't pack. There was about $50.00 in her account. I went to school to pay on the account of two of the other kids. I decided to check her account. I knew she should have at least $50.00 in there. The lady in the cafeteria informed me that she only had $1.80. I thought that was really weird. On my way to the car, it hit me. She was packing her lunch, *and* eating school lunch as well. So, she was eating two lunches a day.

I got home, and called the school. I asked them to have Sarah call me during her lunch break. When she called me I said, "Sarah, something terrible has happened. I went to school, and noticed that your account had only $1.80 in it and it should have about $50.00. I can't imagine what happened to you money. Maybe it was stolen, or they have made a terrible mistake. It couldn't be that you are eating two lunches a day, could it?"

The phone got deathly silent, and then I hear a soft little, "Yes."

I said, "You have been eating two lunches a day?"

She said, "Yes," once again. I told her we would talk about it when she got home.

Tom and I decided to make her pay us back the $48.00 out of her allowance that she spent on the additional lunch. We also zeroed out her account at school, so she couldn't buy lunch the last month of the school year. We explained to her that we had eleven people living in our house. We had 33 meals a day to prepare or pay for, and that we couldn't afford for her to have two lunches a day.

When I got out her allowance envelope, she only had $50.00 in there. It was a painful lesson. Camp was coming up as well as summer vacation, and she wouldn't have as much money to spend. She did have time to save up money so she didn't go without, she just didn't have as much as she would have had. She had to spend her money carefully, so it would last through the summer. Hopefully, it was a lesson learned.

Let's move on to Mike. Mike had trouble with being responsible. I will share three financial lessons that he hopefully learned.

He was on the school baseball team. When it came time to turn his school uniform back in, he couldn't find his. Not only could he not find it, he didn't remember if it was at home, or if he left it at school. He had no clue. We looked high and low for it. We asked his coach if it was found in the school locker room. It never showed up. He had to reimburse the school $25.00 for the cost of the uniform.

The school allowed the kids to check books out of their classrooms. He had checked a book out in his Social Studies class, and at the end of the year, he couldn't find it. We made him pay the $13.00 for the cost of the book.

By the end of paying back his debts, he didn't have enough to buy a new iPod. He had lost his other one.

We had bought Mike a really nice bike, and took the time to get him a nice chain and lock for it. He wanted to ride it to school. One day, we realized he didn't have his bike. We asked where it was. He said it got stolen. We asked how it got stolen, since he had a lock on it, and the place where the bikes were at school was also locked up all day. He informed us that he took his key off his neck and left it on the basketball court. He then came home, and instead of getting his other key and walking back to school to get his bike, he left it there over the weekend, and someone helped themselves to it.

We decided that since he was fourteen, he needed to be responsible for his actions, and so we were not going to buy him another bike. We put a lot of money into that bike fixing it up so it was just like he wanted it. We felt he should have cared enough to get the other key, or at least tell us about it so we could go get it for him. If he wanted another bike, we informed him that he would have to save up his money, and buy it himself.

These are all examples of hard lessons that some of our kids have had to learn. It is not always easy for us to have to teach them these lessons. We feel however, that it is critical that they learn them, so they don't make bigger financial mistakes in the future. These have all been examples of natural consequences. If you spend your money, you don't have any. When you are irresponsible, you pay for your irresponsibility.

When any of the kids break the rules, for example, play their electronic devices when it's lights out, we take away their privilege of playing for the next day. If they are on their phones when their phones should be plugged in, charging for the evening, we take away their phone for a day.

One child was given the privilege of riding their bike to school, but they had to cross several major streets. We found out that they were not crossing at the cross walk, like we had informed them to do, but were instead crossing anywhere they wanted. They lost their privilege of riding their bike to school for a month.

Another child thought it would be fun to ride their bike out in the middle of traffic to see if the big trucks would stop or run them over. It was a game to them. We caught them. To be honest, we were in shock at such stupidity, that it took us a while to figure out what to do. We finally took away anything they had with wheels for quite a while.

Our house rule is that you cannot have any D's on your report card if you want to participate in extracurricular activities. There have been many times that one of our kids has had to sit out during basketball, track, and football season, because of their grades. We try to do everything we can to make sure that doesn't happen, but it doesn't always work. Sometimes, they just have to sit out. Let me give you one example of how we handle grades.

One of the boys came up to me and informed me—three weeks before school was out—that they were failing algebra, but that it was all right, because they can fail three classes and still graduate from high school. I was a little taken aback, because this particular child had lived with me for five years, and I couldn't believe he thought he could pull that excuse off on me.

I said, "What a bummer, because you will have to quit the football team. If you don't get the grades, you don't play."

I then asked him when the problem started, and he said, "Over a month ago."

I asked him why he was just mentioning it, because in the past when he had struggled, we hired him a private tutor to come to the house to help him. He told me that he had been messing around in class, and wasn't really paying attention. So, once again I assured him that I was sad that he would have to give up his varsity football career over one bad grade.

The next day, he was on the computer looking up the assignments that he didn't complete so he could catch them up. On Monday, I called his teacher and asked her what the problem was. She informed me that he was missing tests, daily assignments, and corrected papers, (he was messing around all right). I asked her if there was any way we could get him up to a *C*, because I wanted this to be a lesson for him that you don't fail if you have the ability to succeed. She told me she would be in class every morning at 6:30. If I dropped him off, she would let him make up all his work and re-do his tests.

That night, I told him what the teacher and I had decided he was going to do. He agreed. By the end of the third week of meeting with his teacher, he had a 70% in that class, but at least he didn't fail. He was so excited that he didn't have to give up football, that he was screaming and high-fiving me. We were both dancing around the kitchen that day. I once again went over the lesson for him. Don't fail. That is not who you are. Work hard, take pride in a job well done, and by all means, have a blast playing football!

Let me add, shortly after this incident, I saw him with a piece of construction paper and some crayons. I said, "What are you doing?" He replied, "Making a card for some lady."

I went about my business. Soon after, it was Mother's Day. He handed me a card made out of construction paper. It was what he had been working on earlier. I saved it, because it was so special to me. I just went upstairs to get it out of my hope chest so I could share it word for word with you.

"Happy Mother's Day to the greatest mother in the world, I love you."

Now, I will share what he wrote on the inside of the card....

"Mother, you are too great, and I love you so very much. You are the best mother ever, even though you embarrass me in front of my friends! (I love to do that) You are a great person to be around. You are so funny and strict, sometimes I think too strict, but after I look back at it, I realize what and why you do what you do. It is because you love me. I am so glad you took me to be your son. I can't imagine my life without you. I just want you to know, I am glad you are my mother and I would do anything for you. I love you, Mom. You're the best!"

These kids want to be disciplined in love. They want boundaries. It shows them that you love and care about them. They crave consistency. They know when you are being fair, and when you are not. They know when they deserve to be disciplined. You are doing them an injustice if you don't lovingly teach them through discipline.

We received a call from one of our children's teachers, and they informed us that our child was pretending to masturbate in class. He was grabbing other people, and suggesting that they liked it. The teacher explained to him that it was sexual harassment, and informed him that he could get into a lot of trouble. Those words didn't stop his behavior, so she called us.

When my husband has something difficult to tell me, he always starts with: "Jill, I have something to tell you, and I don't want you to freak out." How nice of him.

He allowed me to hear the voice message from the teacher, and my response was, "Who does that?" I raised two boys, and never had to deal with stuff like this. Anyway, I reminded myself who does that—and that is a foster child who you take in over the age of ten. So, I asked my husband what he was going to do.

He said, "I really have no idea." We slept on it. The next morning, when our child woke up, and we were alone with him in the kitchen, my husband, Tom, asked him if he was feeling brave.

He responded with a, "No."

Tom said, "Really? Because I think you're feeling brave." Tom then took his phone out, put it on speakerphone, and put it up to his ear so he could hear the message from his teacher.

First, our son turned white, then, when Tom asked him what he was thinking, he responded that he wasn't thinking, he was just being stupid.

Tom said, "No, this is *more than stupid*, this is criminal, and if you grabbed one of my children in class—I would file charges on you, and you would have *sexual offender* by your name for years to come."

He then told him that he needed to write an apology letter to his teacher, and assure her his behavior would stop immediately. He had one more athletic game to play before the season was over. My husband said, "After you write the letter, go pack up your sports equipment and take it to your coach, and inform him that you will not be playing in the last game. If he wants to know why, you tell him I have a voice message he can listen to anytime he wants." Well, that was it. Our son broke down crying, but he obeyed.

About a week later, he talked to Tom about it, and said he couldn't believe he was so stupid, and that he really let his dad and his team down. Tom had a good opportunity to spend some time talking with him about it. This is one situation that now we look back on, and crack up. You've got to laugh, or you'll cry!

Tom and I go out every Saturday night for a break. Those evenings are very important to us, and we look forward to them all week. The two girls that babysit our kids have been here for years. They are wonderful, they love the kids, and they get it.

On one of these Saturday nights, one of the boys decided to sneak off with one of his friends from school without telling the sitter. When the sitter noticed he wasn't around, she realized he had taken off with his friend. My girls got out the school directory and got the other boy's phone number. The sitter called it, and our son's friend answered the phone.

She told him to send our son back home. The friend was very disrespectful to the sitter, and she could also hear our son in the background being a smart mouth. The whole situation bothered and frightened her, because a child had never gotten away from her like this before.

When we arrived home, she relayed the events of the evening to us. I went downstairs to his bedroom, woke him up, and made him come upstairs where the three of us were talking.

I said, "Did you take off without telling the sitter?"

He replied, "Yes."

"When she called you did you mouth off to her and disrespect her?"

"Yes."

"When you got home, did you continue to be a smart-mouth to her?"

Again, "Yes."

"Well, let me explain something to you. We give you six nights, and seven days a week of our lives. We care for you, teach you, and give you everything you need. The only thing we ask for in return is one night out alone. "Do you think that is too much to ask?"

"No," he replied.

"Well, let me ask you a few questions. When you're messing with the babysitter, whom are you really messing with?"

He responded, "You."

I said, "Yes, you are. When the babysitter doesn't want to sit with you anymore because of your behavior, then Dad and I won't be able to go out anymore, and that just doesn't seem fair."

I then made him apologize to the sitter and to us, and he assured all of us that it would never happen again. I am happy to say, it hasn't happened again.

Sometimes, a good butt-chewing works well too.

We do try to make the punishment fit the crime. There have been times when I have wanted to kill them, and Tom has wanted to kiss them. We have learned that we are both at opposite ends of the spectrum. Tom and I always try to talk it over, and meet somewhere in the middle—where they are not being killed or kissed. It is not always easy!

A behavioral chart has been known to also work. Let the child work all week to earn a special treat at the end of the week. Have a list of things you would like them to accomplish on a daily basis. If they get a desired amount of stickers for the week, let them pick out the family movie for Friday night family time. Or, in our family, the kids love one-on-one time. So, we take them out on a date with us. That can be a good motivator to get them to accomplish tasks that can be difficult for them.

Our daughter, Joy, can be difficult at times. She has a few fetishes that can get in the way of things. For example, she can't stand a piece of dirt on her body or her clothes. If she is dirty in any way, she changes. She also has a hard time with socks. She turns them inside out, then right-side in, over and over again—on the foot, off the foot. Picking out clothes in the morning is torture. Things have to fit her a certain way, or off they go. There are usually several outfits on the floor that have been cast aside until she finds just the right one to wear.

She used to get me so frustrated, because it took her forever to get ready for school. I was always threatening to discipline her if she didn't get things done. Now, I give her one hour to get ready. That involves getting up, which seems to be the hardest. She needs to eat, comb her hair, get dressed, and brush her teeth.

Every night before bed, I have her get dressed for the next day so when she wakes up one thing is out of the way. I have stopped letting her get to me. I tell her how much time we have before we have to walk out the door. When it is time to leave, there are many times that she has her breakfast, and shoes and socks in her hand to finish up while we drive to school. She knows when I get to school, she is getting out of the car—ready or not. It has worked beautifully. At the last minute, she is finished, and I haven't had to yell.

Of course, there should always be grace given. A child doesn't want to be disciplined every time they make a bad choice. We spend a lot of time talking with them. We try to give grace as often as we give discipline. We want them to know we believe that they can make a better choice, and we want to give them the opportunity to show us they can make good choices. It makes them feel good about themselves, and helps them to be more responsible in the future.

Would we do it all over again?

We are often asked the question, "Would you do it all over again if you knew then what you know now?" It is a question worth answering. I will answer it at the end of the chapter after I fill you in on how the kids are doing now. I also want to share a few cute memories with you.

One day, when Cindy was around the fifth grade, she came home and told me that she had to do a Venn diagram and show the differences and similarities between her and myself. She was so frustrated, because she couldn't think of any differences. I had to laugh. I said, "Well, let's just start here. You're Mexican, and I'm white." Brown eyes, dark hair, long legs—Cindy and I have no physical characteristics that are similar—yet she couldn't think of any. I guess it is true that love is colorblind.

Cindy, my precious daughter who came to us so abused is now 14 years old. "It is beauty that captures your attention, personality which captures your heart." This saying reflects who Cindy is. She is such a blessing, a gift from God, and a breath of fresh air. She has such a sweet spirit and nurturing heart. If you were to drop in our house at dinner, she would jump up and offer you a drink or some food. She never has to be told to see the needs of others. She watches over her younger siblings with a joyful heart. She plays the piano beautifully, and has recently taken up the saxophone. She has played in the hand bell choir, as well as sung in the musical choir. She is also very athletic. She plays on the school volleyball team, has played basketball and softball, and has been in the school plays. She is also a good student.

There is no evidence of her abuse. God has fully and completely healed her! We praise His name for giving us a front row seat to watching this beautiful, precious child come to life! It was one of the greatest miracles I have ever witnessed.

When Mara first came to live with us, Cathy was only three years old. One day we were at the Pediatrician's office. Cathy was admiring a little baby in a car seat. She then asked the mom of the baby, "What a sweet baby. Did you just pick her up at the shelter?" The woman looked at Cathy like she was crazy. I told Cathy that we get our babies at the shelter, but most people go to the hospital to have their babies.

Our oldest son, Matthew, called Cathy a little Mexican once. Cathy informed him that she wasn't a Mexican.

He said, "Yes, you are."

She said, "No, I'm not. I'm white, like you."

He replied, "No, You're a Mexican. Look at your dark skin."

She yelled up at me, "Mom, Matt says I'm a Mexican."

I yelled back, "You are."

She said "Oh, I thought I was white."

We like to have fun regarding their adoption. Tom has told Cathy a fun story about her adoption since she was little. It is not true, she knows it is not true, yet she giggles every time he shares it with her.

He tells her there is a room full of daddies. They are bringing children up on the stage, like an auction, and asking, "Who wants this child?" When Cathy is brought up on stage, they ask who wants this precious, little fat baby. My husband screams, "I do!" But some other daddies say they want her too. He says to the other daddies, "Oh no, you don't, she is mine." He pushes all the other daddies out of the way, and finally after a lot of hard work and a few good punches, he gets to the stage, grabs her, and runs out the door with the other daddies chasing him trying to steal her from him. She loves this story.

Cathy, Cindy's sister, is a hoot, and is 12 years old. "Cute is when a person's personality shines through their looks. Every time you see them, you want to run up and hug them." This is true of Cathy. She is a joy and delight, a bright light on dark days. She is as happy as any kid can be. She is constantly laughing. There are times when we have to ask her to not laugh so loud if you can imagine that. She is very playful, and loves having a good time. She is a social little bunny. She also plays the piano beautifully, but what people comment on most is her voice. I (and others) tell her she sings like an angel. God has given her a tremendous talent, and hopefully she will use that talent for God's glory. She sings in the school choir. She also played hand bells, volleyball, basketball, track, softball, and has been in the school plays. She too is a good student.

There is no evidence of any abuse. God has fully and completely healed her! We praise His name for all the laughter she has brought into our lives. We are so thankful that we have had the opportunity to watch her grow into the beautiful young lady she is today. Every day when we look into her big brown eyes, we are grateful for the immeasurable joy she brings us.

One night, when Mara was seven, Tom was tucking her into bed. She said, "Dad, do you love me maybe *a little bit more* than all the other kids?"

Tom replied, "Yes, Mara, but it's our secret, and you can't tell anyone." She went off to sleep, and when Tom and I were in bed, we laughed about it.

A few nights later, I was tucking Mara into bed and she said to me, "Mom, do you love me *a little bit more* than all the other kids?"

I replied, "Yes, baby, but don't tell anyone that I love you more."

She sat straight up in bed and said, "Well, that is a *sin*. Miss Musser (her first grade teacher) told us that is a sin, and you're not supposed to love one child more than the others."

I said, "Yeah, well, *entrapment* is a sin too—and by the way, I don't love you more." I cracked up. She was so smart even at the age of seven. She got us!

Mara's mother is white, and we think her father must be Mexican-American, because she is dark skinned. She came home from school one day and approached Tom. She said, "Dad, I think I am part Indian." She must have been studying American Natives in school.

Tom said, "Yeah, why?"

She replied very seriously, "Because I don't act a thing like you white people!" Tom just cracked up!

When Mara was about two years old, she was lying in bed drinking some milk with a Sippy cup. My husband went into her room and lay down with her. While he was lying with her, he was telling her how much he loved her and how special she was to him. He was rubbing her little face and really thinking the two of them were sharing a special moment. Mara takes her cup out of her mouth, and looks at Tom and says, "Dad?"

"Yes, baby."

"Get out of my bed." So, he did.

One evening my husband was having a snack of cereal. While he was eating, Mara came up to him and asked for a bite.

He said, "No, you are too stuffed with fluff." He didn't want to share.

To which Mara replied so eloquently, and as only she can, "And that is coming from a man that is over 200 pounds?" My husband decided he didn't have room to talk, and so he gave her a bite and she walked away like she had completed her task.

Mara is nine, and our other rambunctious child. "She can charm the birds out of a tree." She keeps us laughing. She never stops talking, although all her teachers have commented that she never speaks a word during class. I guess she saves that for us. She is always thinking, and loves to sit down with a good book. She loves animals. She runs everywhere she goes, busy as a bee, because she has a purpose. She lives like there is no tomorrow. She is constantly making a mess, because life is all about having fun. She has a pet fish and rabbit that she loves and takes care of. When she is old enough, we are sure she will play school sports. At this time, she has no interest in music.

There is no evidence, and she has no struggles because of her drug addiction and difficult beginning. God has completely healed her! We praise His name for allowing us to be her forever family, and for all the joy and laughter she brings to us on a daily basis!! She is keeping me young—or giving me my gray hair. I am not sure which.

Some of these memories may only be funny to us. One memory that still cracks us up was the day that Joy told Teddy she was going to get a fork and poke his eyes out. Ted was appalled, and we were clapping because Joy put a complete sentence together. We were so proud. It actually had a beginning and an end. We still laugh about that to this day. Ted tells us we had better keep our eye on that one. We say, "It's not *our* eyes she wants to poke out, you better watch out."

Joy is now ten, and our little peanut. She is as delicate as a flower. She is still very small and fragile. She is going to be such a good mom. She loves taking care of babies. She is so nurturing and innocent, and as sweet as honey. She loves to help in the kitchen or help clean up around the house. She still likes to sit on the couch with her blanket and cuddle. She struggles academically, especially in math. She seems to continue to be about two years behind whether it is learning to swim, or riding a bike. Things do not come easy for her.

There is still evidence of Joy's abuse, but we know that all things are possible with God, and that Joy will continue to grow physically, emotionally, and spiritually in the years to come. We praise His name for allowing us to have the honor of watching an infant come to life. We will never forget her first precious laugh, cry, or word spoken! We are blessed beyond measure that this child is our little girl.

David is now 16 years old. He is as sweet as sugar. He is a thankful child who realizes the opportunities he has been given, and is genuinely grateful. He is enjoying life now that he is thin enough to participate in more activities. He is our other social butterfly. He is always hanging out with his friends. He loves playing sports, and participates in as many as he can. He participates in football, wrestling, and track.

He is very sensitive and kind hearted. He has a tender, sweet spirit. He is always thinking of others, and what he can do to help out. He does not hesitate to play with the younger children, especially Mara. He will get on his hands and knees and play horse with her as well as go to her room to play animals. He is protective of all the girls. He is quick-witted, and fun to be around. He has a great sense of humor, and he is fun to tease. He is a very happy young man.

There is no evidence of David's abuse. God has fully and completely healed him! We praise His name for this young man. It has been so much fun to watch him get healthy, and really learn to live life to the fullest. We are so blessed to have had the opportunity to show him that love doesn't hurt, and to have a lot of laughs along the way! Children are a blessing from the Lord, and this young man has certainly blessed our lives immensely.

One time, Paul asked me if ghostes lived in our house. I said, "Ghostes, what are ghostes?"

He replied, "You know they walk around at night with a white sheet over their bodies and holes where their black eyes show through."

I said, "Oh, you mean ghosts. Do ghosts live here?"

Very seriously, he replied, "Yes."

"No," I said, "There are no ghosts in our house."

I thought it was funny because he was about 15 when he asked this question, and he was completely serious. It was one of those moments where I just shook my head, and continued doing dishes. No words were necessary.

Paul is now 19 years old, and getting ready to move out. Because of his disability, things with him don't change much. He is a sweet boy who has a kind heart. He is very compliant, and most of the time he wants to please the people around him. He is an unbelievable artist. Some of his art has already been put on display. It is definitely a God-given talent. He played a school sport for a while, but some sports are mental, and he didn't have the mental capacity to play well so he chose to do other things. He is able to keep a job, and he works hard at it. He is dependable, and a very hard worker. We will probably have to watch over him all his life, but eventually, he should be able to function relatively well on his own with little assistance.

We praise the Lord for allowing us to love this child who we initially saw as something other than a gracious gift from God! He is fearfully and wonderfully made! I think it is amazing that God used this child to teach us—in a more intimate way—about the awesomeness of His creations, and that nothing God does is an accident.

We have a favorite Mexican food restaurant that we take the kids to about once a month. When the kids got old enough to read, they read the sign that said, *Fine Mexican Cuisine*. One of the children yelled out, "This is Mexican food? I thought we were eating Italian food!"

Sarah then commented that the Mexicans have tortillas and enchiladas, the Italians have amazing pasta dishes, and what exactly do we white people have—hamburgers? She shook her head in shame for us white folks.

The kids all attended a private school. In the eighth grade, we moved Sarah to the public school and so she was introduced to a whole new culture. One afternoon, Tom was teasing Cindy, and giving her a hard time. It was all in fun. As Cindy was walking up the stairs she said to Tom, "Dad, I wish you would just stop talking." We cracked up, and Tom said *okay* he would stop talking. There was no disrespect in what she said, she was just playing along.

Sarah was in the kitchen at the time listening to the two of them go back and forth and she said, "I wish I could talk to you that way."

We responded that she could joke around with us anytime she wants.

Her next comment was, "Well, can I tell the two of you to just shut up?"

It was so hilarious. I about died laughing, because she was so serious. I said, "Well, you can, but you aren't going to like the results of that comment, so you will probably only say it once."

She then told me that telling us to *shut up* was nothing compared to what her new friends at school were saying to their parents. So, we had the *I don't care what the other kids say to their parents, we only care about what you say to us* talk. We still laugh about that comment to this day.

Sarah is now 15 years old. She is our serious child, and doesn't have a lot of time for foolishness. When we do hear her laugh (which isn't often), it cracks us all up, because she has such a beautiful laugh. When she chooses to participate in conversation, it is a lot of fun to watch her. She has such a unique personality that she can just crack you up with the things that come out of her mouth.

Her favorite thing to do is study. She is a very good student who can't stand to miss a problem in a class. On the second day of school, she wants me to look up her grades. She has the desire to succeed, and the urge to reach her full potential. When she finishes high school, she wants to further her education and work in the medical field. This would be good for her, because of her love of facts. She also loves to read. She can sit for hours with a good book, and just get lost in it. She can play the piano, and plays the clarinet in the high school marching band. She continues to struggle with her eating disorder, and is still unable to feel empathy for others. We are hopeful that in the future she is able to see and respond to the needs of others.

We praise the Lord for teaching us through her that *odd* is not *odd* to God. She is nothing but perfect in His sight! She is a miracle. Since the beginning of the world, there hasn't been, and until the end of the world there will not be, another child like her. We are grateful that we get to experience this once-in-a-lifetime child, and make her our own.

One day, I rode my bike to the kid's school to pick them up. They had also ridden their bikes to school that day. Mike came across the crosswalk laughing so hard he could hardly breathe. I said, "What is so funny?"

He replied, "My friend told me to tell my grandma that he liked her bike. Mom, he thinks you are my grandma."

I said, "Well, then you have the hottest grandma around." We cracked up all the way home. You have to laugh or you may cry.

Mike is also 15 years old. He is still living in Kentucky with his uncle. He is a very talented young man. He is able to play the guitar and the piano. He excels in all sports. He is an amazing runner, bike rider, wrestler, football player, and anything else he sets his mind to. We gave him a unicycle, and he learned to ride it in one day. All athletics come very easy to him. He is also very smart, and capable of excelling in school if he puts in the work. He has a kind heart. He is able to feel the pain of others, and wants to reach out to them. He also has a love for reading, and can read a 500-page book in a day.

He still struggles with integrity, but with God's help, we believe that he can make a change that is positive, and grow into the wonderful young man we all know he can be.

We praise God for this young man, and the opportunity we have had to pour good things into his life. We are thankful that we plant the seed, and God causes it to grow. We look forward to watching it grow in Mike. He has been a blessing to us because through him, we have learned so much about God's love for us.

Now the answer to the question, "Would we do it all over again?"

The answer is *yes*. When God called us to care for the *least of these*, I never could have imagined what that would entail. If I would have been able to see into the future, I would have been scared out of my mind. But looking back it has been the greatest blessing of my life.

As I was writing this book, there were many times I had to stop because of tears flooding my eyes. We have had so many good memories and fun times. Some of the tears were remembering some of the very difficult times. But, times that have helped us grow as individuals—and as a family.

My husband told me a story he once heard on a talk radio station. It was a station that doesn't give an opinion on the subject matter. They have both sides give their view, and you just get to listen.

The subject matter was "Should gay couples be able to adopt?" After both sides gave their opinion, a caller rang in and was able to share her story. She was now 23, and her sister was 21. They were taken away from their birth family when they were 8 and 6 years old. They jumped from foster home to foster home, never getting adopted. At 18 years of age, they aged out of the system—which means they were on their own.

They now have only each other. She shared that they have nowhere to go for Thanksgiving or Christmas. They have no one to celebrate their birthday with. Nobody is there to help them financially, or give them advice on important or not so important decisions. No one is there to walk them down the aisle on their special day. She felt alone.

Eight beautiful children, who God created, are no longer alone. They have a place to call home. They are loved, cared for, watched over, and given guidance. They have been given opportunities they would have never had. Their children will have grandparents. They have a faith to share and hold onto throughout their life. There is so much that having a family means to a human being, and God intended for all of us to belong and feel safe in a family structure.

Our family, on so many occasions, has been able to experience the faithfulness of God. We have had a front row seat watching God work more than a few miracles in the lives of these kids. Whether it was taking away their fears,

God allowing them to meet a birth parent for the first time, watching them learn to trust, getting to adopt a child who we were told there was no way it could happen, or seeing that light bulb of love come on for the first time in their lives. It has been an incredible journey. We have cried a million tears, and laughed a million more.

I would challenge anyone who has read this book to go out of his or her comfort zone. You may not be called to bring these special children into your home, but you can help in other ways. Step out, trust God, and give love to children who so desperately need to be loved, coddled, and cared about. You will be the one blessed when it is all over.